Elite • 249

Soviet Naval Infantry 1917–91

DAVID GREENTREE

ILLUSTRATED BY JOHNNY SHUMATE

Series editors Martin Windrow & Nick Reynolds

OSPREY PUBLISHING
Bloomsbury Publishing Plc
Kemp House, Chawley Park, Cumnor Hill, Oxford OX2 9PH, UK
29 Earlsfort Terrace, Dublin 2, Ireland
1385 Broadway, 5th Floor, New York, NY 10018, USA
E-mail: info@ospreypublishing.com
www.ospreypublishing.com

OSPREY is a trademark of Osprey Publishing Ltd

First published in Great Britain in 2023

A catalogue record for this book is available from the British Library.

ISBN: PB 9781472851628; eBook 9781472851635;
ePDF 9781472851611; XML 9781472851604

23 24 25 26 27   10 9 8 7 6 5 4 3 2 1

Index by Rob Munro
Typeset by PDQ Digital Media Solutions, Bungay, UK
Printed and bound in India by Replika Press Private Ltd.

Osprey Publishing supports the Woodland Trust, the UK's leading woodland
conservation charity.

To find out more about our authors and books visit
www.ospreypublishing.com. Here you will find extracts, author
interviews, details of forthcoming events and the option to sign up for
our newsletter.

Front cover, above: Soviet naval infantry during the defence of Sevastopol,
April 1942. (Sovfoto/Universal Images Group via Getty Images)

Title-page photograph: This painting depicts sailors during the Kronstadt
Rebellion of March 1921. These men wear the *telnyashka* blue-and-white
striped undershirt and the white flannel shirt worn during the summer
months, with a separate blue collar edged with three white stripes. Such a
uniform would not be worn during March 1921 when Kronstadt was
experiencing a harsh winter. (Universal History Archive/Universal Images
Group via Getty Images)

CONTENTS

SOVIET NAVAL INFANTRY 1917–91

ORIGINS

The Russian naval infantry has a long tradition dating back to the 16th century when *Streltsy*, men equipped with early forms of musket, would be brought on board warships. During the 17th century, Russian warships carried soldiers whose duties would be to board enemy ships. The first regiment was formed in November 1705 for boarding and landing operations against Swedish forces, but it was disbanded after the end of the Great Northern War (1700–21) and replaced with five battalions drawn from Imperial Russian Army personnel. These units were used against the Ottomans and by 1782 eight battalions had been formed. By 1811, in the midst of the Napoleonic Wars (1803–15), the Army took charge of the battalions, and by the 1840s the naval infantry were incorporated into the Army. During the Crimean War (1853–56), 17 battalions of Imperial Russian Navy sailors defended Sevastopol during the siege by British, Ottoman and French forces. These were not permanent formations, however, and they were disbanded when the Crimean War ended. Similarly, seven battalions of sailors were formed during the Russo-Japanese War (1904–05), and were engaged in the defence of Port Arthur.

The Imperial Russian Navy established a small number of permanent naval-infantry units in the years before 1914. At the beginning of World War I, the Baltic Fleet had two battalions based at Kronstadt on Kotlin Island in the Gulf of Finland, with a third soon formed from a cadre of sailors from the 1st Battalion plus elements from the Guards Equipage Battalion; a fourth battalion was formed with sailors from the 2nd Battalion. Each battalion had a total strength of 550 men. They trained for amphibious landings, but would support few of the landings the Army made. In August 1914 the Navy also had a naval-infantry battalion based at Kerch on the Kerch Peninsula (linking the Sea of Azov with the Black Sea), plus two battalions at Batumi on the Black Sea and a detachment and company at Baku on the Caspian Sea. By early 1917 these units, together with Army personnel, would form a division. The Baltic Fleet also formed a naval-infantry division, based on the battalions it had established.

After the February Revolution of 1917 these naval-infantry units were quickly disbanded; but when politicians and military planners looked abroad, the Navy took on a greater importance, as did the naval infantry. When the leaders focused on domestic issues, however, the opposite was true. The debate about whether the Army or Navy should form and control naval-infantry formations continued until 1945.

Formed in 1810, the Guards Equipage Battalion was a naval-infantry unit, shown here during the February Revolution of 1917 heading to the Tauride Palace in Petrograd (modern-day St Petersburg). Most of the battalion's personnel were at the front line and troops occupying barracks were training formations. The battalion would declare loyalty to the Imperial State Duma, which used the Tauride Palace for meetings. (Courtesy of the Central Museum of the Armed Forces, Moscow via Stavka)

SAILORS IN THE RUSSIAN CIVIL WAR

ORGANIZATION AND EQUIPMENT

After their assumption of power in Russia in November 1917, the Bolsheviks deployed some 100,000 sailors as infantry in 1917–20. Units formed from naval personnel were ad hoc, scratch forces, equipped with whatever weapons could be found, typically the same as those used by the Red Army; in fact, the sailors gained a reputation for carrying as much weaponry and ammunition as they could, doubtless to allay problems of resupply when on operations.

OPERATIONS

The sailors' first struggle would be against the Don Cossack forces occupying Ukraine. Having lost their former privileges, many mounted units of Cossacks fought against the Bolsheviks. Crimean sailors fought against Cossacks at Rostov-on-Don, a traditional centre of Cossack power. Initially successful, the Bolshevik sailors soon ran out of ammunition; the city was lost to the Cossacks on 15 December 1917. Another detachment of sailors was sent to fight the Cossack force headed by General Lavr Georgiyevich Kornilov, the former commander-in-chief of the Imperial Russian Army. Kornilov's contingent,

Sailors congregate around a motor car; their cap bands bear the names of their ships, a practice that gave way to displaying the name of the fleet by the time of the Great Patriotic War. Their slung Mosin-Nagant rifles are not fitted with bayonets, presumably to avoid hampering the users' movements during policing activities. The sailor wearing a cap on the back of his head and an open pea jacket represented the classic image of the Russian Civil War; the first detachments of sailors would establish Soviet power and break the first anti-Soviet demonstrations. Wearing distinctive uniforms and physically fit, the sailors made a strong impression. (Courtesy of the Central Museum of the Armed Forces, Moscow via Stavka)

Greatcoated sailors wearing the flat, visorless cap called the *beskozyrka* conduct a patrol in Petrograd, October 1917; the man at right in the front row wears the *bashlyk*, a cold-weather hood that could be wrapped around the neck like a scarf. Initially, the Bolshevik regime could not do without the sailors, whether to counter German aggression or to deal with counter-revolutionaries. Some, however, outraged at the Peace of Brest-Litovsk and the authoritarianism of the Bolsheviks, conducted anti-Soviet riots and terrorist attacks. The deliberate destruction of the Black Sea Fleet on 18 June 1918 further disillusioned them. The Bolsheviks began to disband sailor detachments, disperse them or subordinate them to Army units. Commissars were appointed to discourage democratic ideas and teach Bolshevism. Some of the sailors' leaders accepted this process while others attempted to retain the ideals they had fought for and would disappear fighting as members of anarchist or peasant groups. (Keystone/Getty Images)

some 3,600 soldiers who were mainly former Imperial Russian Army officers wanting to unite with the Cossacks, was defeated at Belgorod by the sailors with support from Red Army detachments.

Mensheviks, some of whom supported opposition to the Bolsheviks, formed a Crimean People's Republic. When ships with sailors sympathetic to the Bolsheviks deployed from Sevastopol to fight the Cossacks, the port city was left poorly defended. In January 1918 the Crimean forces attacked, but sailors from the battleship *Potemkin* stopped them on the city's approaches; they then took Simferopol in conjunction with Army units and mass arrests took place. Sailors then deployed to Evpatoria, defeating other groups of Cossacks and shooting the leaders. At Rostov-on-Don, eight ships landed 510 sailors and the city was temporarily occupied for the Bolsheviks.

Bolshevik authority was then threatened by the establishment of a Ukrainian People's Republic. The Ukrainian Republic's army fought against the sailors of the Odessa naval base, who were supported by 7,000 volunteers and Bolshevik-minded soldiers of the Army garrison. By mid-January 1918, sailors from the cruiser *Almaz* seized key locations and made senior officers prisoner, quickly bringing the city under Bolshevik control.

A SAILORS DEPLOYED AS INFANTRY DURING THE RUSSIAN CIVIL WAR

(1) Officer, Baltic Fleet

This former *stárshiy leytenánt* (senior lieutenant) wears a pea jacket and peaked cap. Rank insignia was abolished by the Bolsheviks. He is equipped with a 7.62mm Nagant M1895 seven-round revolver, the standard-issue sidearm used by Russian officers; it remained in service throughout World War II. The revolver is attached to the officer's holster by a lanyard. He is also equipped with a naval dirk.

(2) Sailor, Baltic Fleet

This sailor wears a flannel shirt with the *telnyashka* undershirt showing at the neck. The Imperial Russian Navy adopted the *telnyashka* during the late 19th century and it remained a mark of the naval infantry – and the Soviet airborne forces – until 1991, and has continued in the present-day Russian military as a mark of elite status. A red star has been fitted to his cap in place of the Imperial Russian Navy insignia. He has his 7.62mm M1891 Mosin-Nagant bolt-action rifle slung; the sling attachment ring dates the rifle's manufacture to before 1898. A socket bayonet with long spike blade was used; a bayonet scabbard was not issued as servicemen were expected to keep the bayonet permanently fitted. A pair of cartridge cases are attached to his waist belt, and he is carrying an M1910 ammunition box with belts of 250 cartridges.

(3) PM M1910 gunner, Baltic Fleet

This sailor, a former crew member on the destroyer *Azard*, has retained the Imperial Russian Navy brass buckle showing the Imperial eagle but wears a red armband signifying his allegiance to the Bolshevik cause. He carries a 7.62mm M1895 Nagant revolver for personal defence. The water-cooled 7.62mm PM M1910 MMG weighed a formidable 64.3kg, but remained in Russian and Soviet service for decades; it can still be seen in some parts of the world.

Anatoly Grigorievich Zheleznyakov was a typical sailor who supported the Bolsheviks. A dockyard worker who joined the Baltic Fleet during World War I, he deserted when he was discovered to be distributing anti-government propaganda. He was elected to the Tsentrobalt, the Congress of the Baltic Fleet, by May 1917. He participated in the October Revolution of 1917, helping to storm the Winter Palace in Petrograd, and was appointed to the Naval Revolutionary Committee to organize the formation of sailor detachments. By February 1918 he was sent to Odessa, leading a special detachment of sailors defending the approaches to the city. He commanded Army units by June 1918, though not without problems with other officers. Following arguments with his commander he would be dismissed and by October was sent to Odessa to work underground. He was killed on 26 July 1919 while fighting forces commanded by Lieutenant-General Denikin. (UtCon Collection/Alamy Stock Photo)

On 18 February 1918, German forces seeking to eject Bolshevik forces from Ukrainian territory targeted Odessa in cooperation with Ukrainian forces. Contingents of Bolshevik sailors sent from Crimea were defeated, but some like the detachment led by Warrant Officer V. Lyashchenko, did not surrender, fighting to the end on 13 March. While the Bolsheviks had occupied Kiev by early February, German and Austro-Hungarian forces threw them out by early March 1918. Ukrainian independence was recognized by the Peace of Brest-Litovsk, signed by Germany and Russia on 3 March; but though peace was signed, the Germans continued to attack, reaching Kherson on 20 March. A popular uprising and sailors from Crimea helped throw the Germans back, but success was only temporary; on 6 April, 20,000 German troops took the city again, then stormed through Crimea to seize Sevastopol on 30 April. The sailors based at Sevastopol had not complied with the peace accords, however, supporting operations against German soldiers. The Germans demanded the surrender of Sevastopol but by early May the Russian ships at Sevastopol had escaped to Novorossiysk on the Kuban Peninsula on the Black Sea. By June, this port was also threatened and the Germans demanded that the Russian ships go back to Crimea. Lenin stated that the ships should be sunk and most would be scuttled; 2,000 sailors from the ships' crews went to the front.

Sailors based at ports in Ukraine adopted policies including the shooting of officers and bourgeoisie to create the dictatorship of the proletariat. Some naval units would be disbanded through the middle of 1918 when more Red Army units were established. When World War I came to an end in November 1918, many sailors thought world revolution was about to occur. The attempt to incite a Bolshevik uprising in Estonia failed, however, and soon ended this belief.

Following the defeat of Germany, the Entente Powers took control of Crimea. By early 1919, Bolshevik forces were again sent to Ukraine and on 5 February, Kiev was temporarily occupied. From early June, another serious threat to the Bolsheviks materialized. Having assumed command of Kornilov's army following his death on 13 April 1918, Lieutenant-General Anton Ivanovich Denikin commenced a highly successful offensive that summer, seizing the Kuban. By mid-1919 he was pushing on to Moscow from Ukraine.

Petrograd was also threatened when the coastal fortress at Krasnaya Gorka on the southern shore of the Gulf of Finland was occupied by the Entente Powers following a naval mutiny. On 15 June 1919, however, 4,500 sailors formed the Coastal Group of Forces and took the fortress back. By September, former Imperial Russian Army officer General Nikolai Nikolayevich Yudenich opened another front by attacking Petrograd from Estonia with 17,000 men; guns on ships and coastal batteries helped to stop him. Although Yudenich's forces had reached the suburbs of Petrograd by 19 October, he could not cut the railway line from Moscow, along which the Bolsheviks brought reinforcements and stalled his attack. The Estonians would intern Yudenich's army when the Bolsheviks recognized Estonian independence with the signing of the Treaty of Dorpat on 2 February 1920.

Denikin had been defeated at Orel in October 1919; by March 1920 his withdrawing forces had reached Crimea. By April, Denikin had resigned and Lieutenant-General Pyotr Nikolayevich Wrangel replaced him. With Polish support, the Ukrainian Republic's forces captured Kiev from the Bolsheviks by early May, only to be ejected by a Bolshevik counter-attack. Capitalizing on this opportunity, Wrangel also sent 8,000 men commanded

Sailors of the Baltic Fleet, May 1919. By late 1917 only 50 per cent of Baltic Fleet sailors stayed on, the others heading home or to other fronts, with Lenin sending 2,000 to Ukraine on 15 January 1918. The Baltic Fleet sailors joined the Crimean sailors led by former Baltic Fleet sailor Alexey Vasilievich Mokrousov, forming a unit of 2,600 men. A detachment of 450 sailors commanded by Nikolai Alexandrovich Khovrin and equipped with two armoured trains, four armoured vehicles and 40 machine guns was sent to Kharkov. They fought at Belgorod and would start to eliminate political opponents. Most of the detachment returned to Petrograd and dispersed demonstrations supporting the Constituent Assembly. (Universal History Archive/Universal Images Group via Getty Images)

by Lieutenant-General Sergei Georgievich Ulagay to attack southern Ukraine from Crimea. On 25 August 1920, Ulagay's contingent was defeated on the Kuban Peninsula by the Bolsheviks' 1st Marine Expeditionary Division, which had landed by sea; by August, Ulagay was forced to evacuate to Crimea.

The armistice between the Poles and Bolsheviks allowed the Bolsheviks to turn on Wrangel during October 1920 and he was thrown out of Crimea the following month. Sailors contributed to this success. Yet despite others from Kronstadt and the Caspian being sent to support the 1st Marine Expeditionary Division, Wrangel managed to defeat the sailors and on 20 October they were pulled out of the line and their units disbanded.

Although at first Lenin would trust the sailors with imposing order, once the Bolshevik regime had largely defeated its opponents, it sought to decrease the role played by the sailors. Many sailors were disillusioned by the increasing authoritarianism of the Bolsheviks and the peace signed with Germany would outrage them. Many responded by departing for southern Russia, joining anti-Bolshevik rioters or anarchist groups or leaving Russia for good. While sailors of the Baltic Fleet were employed to establish naval forces under direct orders from Moscow, the Bolsheviks disbanded other sailor detachments or subordinated them to the Red Army. Commissars were assigned to discourage independent political participation among the sailors.

Once the Bolsheviks had prevailed over the counter-revolutionary forces led by Denikin and others, workers and peasants led a campaign to end the hated War Communism. This policy mandated the appropriation of agricultural surplus and militarized labour. Sailors thought the policy would be ended when the Russian Civil War (1917–22) was won, but instead Lenin's regime tightened its grip. This led to peasant uprisings and food shortages, the workers in Petrograd protesting when the authorities banned them from trading with the peasants. In March 1921, the sailors at Kronstadt decided to support the Petrograd workers; but the sailors should have waited until the spring thaw. By storming the base immediately, the Bolshevik regime put an end to the uprising: 2,000 perpetrators would be shot, something shocking to most Bolsheviks. The secret police quickly took hostage many sailors' family members and rounded up leaders of the workers' protests.

NAVAL INFANTRY 1922–41

STRATEGY AND DOCTRINE

Communist theory taught that communist states could not co-exist harmoniously with capitalist states and that war was inevitable. Consequently, a rapid industrialization through the 1930s was deemed necessary to strengthen the Soviet Union's defences. In order to resist a land invasion by potential enemies, the Red Army would raise mobile formations equipped with tanks and towed artillery. The Soviet Navy would play a secondary role. Ships' guns and coastal batteries would be used to support the Red Army. Naval personnel would hold bases and support ground units by organizing infantry units.

The weakened fleets of the Soviet Navy needed to be rebuilt, but this could only happen once a proper industrial base and modern shipbuilding facilities had been established. The construction of large surface vessels such as battleships in order to create an ocean-going fleet had to be delayed until this work was completed, and would be ongoing at the time of the German invasion of the Soviet Union in June 1941. Instead, the Soviet Union focused on building smaller ships for coastal operations of limited scope.

Moreover, senior leadership for the Soviet Navy was also lacking because 80 per cent of naval captains were executed during the brutal purges of the 1930s, the primary intention of which was to ensure loyalty to Stalin's regime but also to expedite a battleship-building programme that was destined to fail by the start of the Great Patriotic War (1941–45). Insufficient resources and personnel would be set aside during the late 1930s to develop the most effective coastal fleet forces; and a lack of sufficiently experienced commanders needed to operate and staff the fleet would hamper its operational effectiveness.

By 1941 the Soviet Navy had established the Baltic, Black Sea, Northern and Pacific Fleet commands; but Soviet Navy ships could not operate offensively at the start of the Great Patriotic War. Instead, the construction of smaller maritime assets intended for limited coastal operations would be the Soviet Navy's priority. Projection of power beyond the immediate coastal zone around Soviet territory was not needed, and neither was naval infantry. In this analysis, amphibious operations would be carried out by the Red Army, and did not require the existence of a specially trained naval force. Landing from boats on an enemy-occupied coast was specified by Soviet Navy doctrine, but its implementation had yet to be addressed.

A Soviet Navy parade. The officer at left is a *komandir korablya 2 ranga* (ship commander 2nd grade), while the enlisted man at front right is a *stárshiy botsman* (senior boatswain); the others in the front rank bear the rank of *komandir otdeleniya* (section commander). By 1924, only 562,000 Red Army and Soviet Navy personnel would remain in uniform, with soldiers making up about 85 per cent and sailors the rest. Komsomol youth organization members needed to be encouraged to join the Soviet Navy. (Archiv Gerstenberg/ullstein bild via Getty Images)

Pictured in February 1938, this sailor wears a cap that suggests he is with the Amur Military Flotilla, based near Manchuria. He is probably manning his PM M1910 MMG on a patrol boat. (Hulton Archive/Getty Images)

ORGANIZATION AND EQUIPMENT

As World War II took hold in Europe in late 1939, the Soviet Union had only just begun to rebuild the naval infantry with the formation of the 1st Separate Rifle Brigade. Numbering some 6,000 all ranks, this brigade was redesignated the 1st Naval Infantry Brigade on 25 April 1940. It had a battalion of 76mm guns, and a tank company with 20 T-26 light tanks. The four rifle battalions each had supporting 76mm and 45mm gun batteries.

OPERATIONS

The newly formed Soviet naval infantry was blooded fighting against the Finns during the Winter War (1939–40). During late February 1940, the 1st Separate Rifle Brigade committed its 3rd Battalion, which together with a battalion of sailors on skis supported Red Army units in capturing the Koivisto Islands in the Gulf of Finland. On 4 March, the Soviet operation to turn the Mannerheim Line commenced; the 3rd Battalion and the sailor ski battalion seized the islands of Huovari and Pitkyaluoto in the teeth of strong Finnish opposition, as part of a larger operation to distract the enemy. The deception was a success, and the naval infantry withstood a strong Finnish counter-attack.

In 1940, the newly established naval infantry were also engaged in Estonia. Having gained independence from Russia in 1918, Estonia successfully defended this independence during the Russian Civil War. The Molotov–Ribbentrop Pact of August 1939 assigned Estonia to the Soviet sphere of influence, however. After German and Soviet forces occupied Poland, Moscow sent an ultimatum to Tallinn demanding that 25,000 Soviet soldiers be stationed on Estonia's territory while World War II continued: the Estonian government agreed; but on 16 June 1940, the Soviet Union attacked Estonia with a force numbering 90,000 men. The 1st Naval Infantry Brigade deployed four battalions on transport ships during the operation; the brigade's 76mm and 45mm artillery guns had tractors and were also deployed. Troops from the brigade occupied the islands of Naissaar, north-west of Tallinn, and Aegna, located in Tallinn Bay; other ships landed troops directly at Tallinn harbour. The Estonian Defence Force was told not to fight as resistance was considered futile. Some skirmishes on Tallinn's streets soon ended with the Estonians negotiating a surrender.

T-37A amphibious light tanks cross a river, 29 October 1941. The lack of armoured support for Soviet amphibious landing forces would soon become apparent. The T-37A was used for scouting, especially by units operating in swampy terrain such as that encountered in Karelia when fighting the Finns, but its issue to reconnaissance units of Red Army rifle and tank formations was suspended before Operation *Barbarossa* began on 22 June 1941. Lightly armoured and equipped only with a single 7.62mm DT machine gun, the T-37A would see limited use in river assaults, sometimes supporting Red Army rifle formations rather than naval-infantry formations. (AirSeaLand Photos)

NAVAL INFANTRY IN THE GREAT PATRIOTIC WAR

STRATEGY AND DOCTRINE

Operation *Barbarossa*, the Axis invasion of the Soviet Union that commenced on 22 June 1941, saw a change of focus in 1942 as the Germans, having initially harnessed their formidable mobility, armour and air assets to encircle and defeat vast numbers of Red Army personnel, switched from targeting major communication hubs and political centres to seizing the Soviet Union's economic assets, ranging from the oilfields of the Caucasus to the Murmansk railway in the north. This change of emphasis shifted the focus of military activity to the coasts of the Soviet Union, thus foregrounding the naval infantry's potential contribution to the Soviet war effort.

From the beginning of the Great Patriotic War, Soviet naval infantry would earn a reputation for tough defence of ports and cities near the coast.

Sailors aboard a motorboat prepare to disembark. During the Great Patriotic War, the Soviet Navy would assist the Red Army by conducting amphibious operations using naval infantry. Most would be raids by brigade-strength forces. During a major landing, elements of naval-infantry brigades frequently went ashore jointly with Red Army ground forces and would be deployed with the first echelon. When operating independently, the naval infantry usually landed at two or three designated locations, depending on the terrain and the strength of enemy defences, on a frontage 800–1,000m wide, organized as two echelons with artillery group and reserve. (Nik Cornish at www.stavka.org.uk)

They would also conduct tactical and operational-sized amphibious landings. At first, most of these landings were small, carried out by a battalion or brigade, but they played an important role by diverting the German forces from the main axis of advance, thus buying more time for Soviet ground forces to regroup. Later, especially from 1943, the naval infantry would help breach Axis defences near the coast, seize bridgeheads for follow-on ground forces, and capture enemy ports and bases; but perhaps the greatest contribution they made was the supply of manpower necessary to support the ground war: 389,975 sailors operated as infantry during June 1941–May 1943, with another 100,000 being added up to the war's end. Most of the naval brigades or battalions they joined would be identifiable as Soviet Navy units, but some sailors would join established Red Army units.

A *stárshiy leytenánt* (senior lieutenant) on a warship explains the plan of attack to beret-clad sailors. Landings would be hastily organized and orders concentrated on getting the naval infantry to the landing areas, not on the formation and consolidation of beachheads. Tactical amphibious landings intended to slow the Axis invaders by diverting their forward momentum would be made by the naval infantry throughout 1941. (Nik Cornish at www.stavka.org.uk)

WARTIME EXPANSION

Germany's invasion of the Soviet Union prompted a rapid expansion of the naval infantry: a total of 19 naval-infantry brigades, 13 regiments and 70-plus battalions or companies were formed and 500,000 sailors would fight on land.

The Northern Fleet formed a single naval-infantry brigade in 1941, the 12th, with three battalions in being by September of that year; by October the 4th and 5th battalions had joined the brigade, with the 6th Battalion joining by the end of 1941 and the 7th Battalion by early 1942. In July 1942, the 254th Naval Infantry Brigade was formed by the Northern Fleet from the 135th Rifle Regiment (14th Rifle Division), serving until it was disbanded in mid-1944.

The Baltic Fleet would contribute 125,000 personnel by the end of the Great Patriotic War, serving in a total of nine naval-infantry brigades. In July–September 1941, seven new brigades (the 2nd, 3rd, 4th, 5th, 6th and 7th, plus a cadet brigade) plus seven separate battalions and many detachments were formed to join the existing 1st Naval Infantry Brigade; these would be joined by the 260th Naval Infantry Brigade in July 1942 (see below).

The Pacific Fleet would contribute 143,407 personnel by mid-1943. By February 1942, the 13th and 14th Naval Infantry brigades were in being, and were joined by the 15th Naval Infantry Brigade in April that year. By February 1943, however, the 14th and 15th Naval Infantry brigades had been disbanded and their personnel sent to other units at the front. As for the 13th Naval Infantry Brigade, composed of the 74th, 75th, 76th, 77th and 78th battalions plus the 390th SMG Battalion, it was deployed on combat operations during 1945 only.

By the end of 1942, the Black Sea Fleet had contributed 50,000 personnel, rising to a total of 57,197 by the war's end. They formed seven naval-infantry brigades as well as some separate regiments and battalions. The 6th Naval Infantry Brigade, composed of the 14th and 35th battalions, was formed at Novorossiysk by August 1941, but the brigade headquarters was disbanded by late September. The 7th Naval Infantry Brigade, 5,210 strong

A Soviet Navy *kapitan 2-go ranga* (captain 2nd rank) addresses rifle-equipped sailors wearing a mix of caps and helmets. While displaying great courage, naval infantry would lack basic infantry training, and the wearing of soft caps rather than helmets led to unnecessary casualties. Formation of units would be haphazard. The pace of the German forces' advance in the Soviet Union was so rapid that headquarters and bases had to improvise using the personnel and equipment immediately at their disposal; when bases were threatened by enemy ground forces, those personnel not manning ships would be hastily cobbled together to form units. When some time to organize more thoroughly was available, however, naval-infantry brigades were formed by the various fleets. (Courtesy of the Central Museum of the Armed Forces, Moscow via Stavka)

and composed of four battalions, was formed at Sevastopol by October 1941 and would defend that city; the 8th Naval Infantry Brigade was likewise formed by October, with four battalions being shipped to Sevastopol from Novorossiysk. The 9th Naval Infantry Brigade was formed at Kerch with four battalions from August 1941 to defend the base by late October. The brigade was re-formed by December that year from mostly new recruits assigned to ships based at Taganrog on the Sea of Azov. The Black Sea Fleet's 1st Naval Infantry Brigade, composed of the 14th, 142nd and 322nd battalions formed by the North Caucasus Military District during August 1942, was re-named the 255th Naval Infantry Brigade by September that year. Also formed by August 1942, the 2nd Naval Infantry Brigade was composed of the 16th, 144th and 305th battalions; on 22 August it was disbanded and the battalions joined the 83rd Naval Infantry Brigade.

ORGANIZATION

By the end of 1941, the majority of Soviet Navy sailors fighting as ground forces were organized either as *Morskoy pekhota* (naval infantry) or *Morskaya strelkovaya* (naval rifle) brigades. While naval-infantry brigades were supposed to be used on combat operations near the coast, the naval-rifle brigades were to be used on the land front.

Each naval-infantry brigade, to start with at least, was typically composed of 4–6 infantry battalions, an artillery battalion (12 76mm guns), a sapper company, a reconnaissance company and service units. Each battalion was supposed to be composed of three rifle companies (each with three rifle platoons, a light-mortar section and a medium-machine-gun (MMG) section), a machine-gun company (12 MMGs and 120 men), a mortar company (16 82mm mortars), an artillery company (four 76mm guns) and an anti-tank platoon (two 45mm guns). Each rifle platoon was composed of four sections each with two NCOs and ten enlisted men equipped with a light machine gun (LMG) and rifles. An anti-tank rifle (ATR) company (three platoons, each with six ATRs) would be added to the brigade strength by early 1942. From 1942–43, some brigades received another mortar company (12 120mm mortars), a separate anti-tank battalion (12 45mm guns), a submachine-gun (SMG) battalion (640 men) and a sapper battalion rather than a sapper company.

As the Northern Fleet had no landing ships assigned to it in 1941–42, the artillery assets of its 12th Naval Infantry Brigade were limited to 82mm mortars and 45mm guns. By June 1943 the brigade was composed of four infantry battalions, each with three rifle companies, a machine-gun company and a 120mm mortar company, plus a single artillery battalion (12 76mm guns), an anti-tank battalion (12 45mm guns), a signals battalion with two signals companies, an SMG company and a reconnaissance company.

On 18 October 1941, a decree stipulated the formation of 25 naval-rifle brigades with another eight to follow. Of the 108,350 personnel required, 37,287 would be sailors, mostly from the Black Sea and Pacific fleets, with smaller contingents raised from headquarters and training establishments and the Amur and Caspian Sea flotillas. These brigades would operate mostly on the land fronts.

Numbering 4,334 all ranks, the naval-rifle brigade fielded three rifle battalions; each of these had three rifle companies plus a machine-gun company (88 men with 16 MMGs and eight wagons). Each rifle company had four platoons, each of which had four sections. Each section had two

NCOs and ten enlisted men equipped with an LMG and rifles. Rifle battalions lacked a mortar company, but at brigade level a mortar battalion with eight 82mm and 16 120mm mortars was available. The battalion headquarters had SMG, scout and signals platoons.

The naval-rifle brigade also had an anti-tank battalion (12 anti-tank guns), a mortar battalion (eight 82mm and 16 120mm mortars), an artillery battalion (eight, later 12, 76mm guns), an SMG company (three platoons, each with three sections of ten men), an ATR company (four platoons, each of four sections, with 48 ATRs in total), a sapper company (three platoons, each of four sections), a reconnaissance company (two platoons, each of two sections) and a truck company. The ATR company was later incorporated into the anti-tank battalion; each rifle battalion would also get a platoon of eight ATRs.

WEAPONS AND EQUIPMENT

The 7.62mm Mosin-Nagant M91/30 bolt-action rifle was the basic infantry weapon; sailors were also issued the 7.62mm SVT-40 semi-automatic rifle. Submachine guns were popular, notably the 7.62mm PPSh-41 and from 1943 the 7.62mm PPS-43. Sailors had the RGD-33 anti-personnel fragmentation stick grenade, supplemented by the RG-42 anti-personnel fragmentation hand grenade by 1942, and the smaller F-1 anti-personnel fragmentation hand grenade; RPG-40, RPG-43 and RPG-6 anti-tank hand grenades would be used against enemy armour. The 7.62mm DP was the section LMG, while machine-gun companies had the 7.62mm PM M1910 wheeled MMG with gun shield and fed with 250-round ammunition belts. The lighter 7.62mm SG-43 MMG, also on a wheeled mount, was issued from 1943. The 12.7mm DShK 1938 HMG would hardly be used by the sailors.

The naval infantry used mortars extensively as they could be transported easily. While the 50mm RM-40 or RM-41 had a range of 800m, the 82mm PM-41 had a 3,040m range and the 120mm M1938 could attain 5,900m. Like the Red Army, the naval infantry used two types of ATR; the 14.5mm round fired from the single-shot PTRD and the semi-automatic PTRS could penetrate 40mm of armour at 100m. The M-42 anti-tank gun's 45mm shell could penetrate 71mm at the same range, while the 57mm ZIS-2 issued to naval-rifle brigades could pierce 90mm. Artillery battalions of naval-infantry brigades operated mainly 76mm M1927 and later M1943 infantry-support guns, with naval-rifle brigades using 76mm M1939 and later M1942 guns.

A small tank battalion, usually fielding the T-26 light tank armed with a 45mm gun and two 7.62mm machine guns, could be part of a naval-infantry

During the winter of 1941/42, sailors formed units on skis when it was necessary to manoeuvre rapidly on snow. An M1910 MMG could also be carried easily on a sled, as demonstrated here. On 10 December 1941, the 64th Naval Rifle Brigade formed a group of 600 skiers to intercept the withdrawal of German columns from Klin at Solnechnogorsk; the brigade then took Troitskoye and then Volokolamsk on 20 December. (Courtesy of the Central Museum of the Armed Forces, Moscow via Stavka)

Sailors armed with slung PPSh-41 SMGs and wearing M1943 tunics move through Sevastopol, May 1944. By April 1943, naval-rifle battalions equipped one-third of their personnel with SMGs. Some battalions organized an SMG platoon per rifle company, some an SMG company per battalion and some an SMG section per platoon. By late 1943, some naval-infantry and naval-rifle brigades had an SMG battalion with three SMG companies (each with 90 SMGs, four ATRs and two LMGs) and a machine-gun company with 151 men (equipped with 118 SMGs, 20 rifles, ten LMGs, two MMGs and three mortars), plus a sapper platoon and a reconnaissance platoon. (Sovfoto/Universal Images Group via Getty Images)

brigade's organization. These were local phenomena and depended on the tanks found locally. Some brigades established by the Baltic Fleet during 1941 might have received KV-1 heavy tanks from the Kirov plant before it was relocated beyond the Urals.

Naval-rifle brigades certainly worked closely with tank brigades equipped with the KV-1 or the T-34 medium tank, especially during the Soviet counter-offensive of winter 1941/42, and so the naval-rifle brigades might well have operated some of the same types of tanks. While the KV-1's 90mm of frontal armour and 75mm of side armour made it invulnerable to German anti-tank guns before the summer of 1942, the faster T-34 had 60mm of frontal armour and 40mm of side armour; both types were equipped with a 76.2mm main gun and three or four 7.62mm machine guns.

Few trucks were used by the naval infantry. A naval-rifle brigade had trucks for its anti-tank and signals battalions; a truck company was also part of the brigade's organization to be utilized as the commander thought fit. Artillery, mortar and machine-gun units used horse-drawn wagons. The naval-infantry brigade had only a truck company, and no horses or wagons assigned. The ZIS-5 4×2 truck was probably the most common, capable of carrying 25 men or a 3-ton cargo.

A lack of specialized landing craft would hamper the Soviet naval infantry's ability to put assault forces ashore successfully. The naval infantry embarked on a host of ships ranging from trawlers, minesweepers, patrol boats, and larger warships. Submarine chasers were used extensively because their armament could be used to support a landing and they had room to accommodate 20–40 men on deck depending on type. Equipped with two 45mm 21K guns and two 12.7mm DShK HMGs, the MO-4-series submarine chasers could achieve speeds of 27kn (50km/h); range was 367nmi (680km) at 15kn (28km/h), and 219 would be built by the end of the Great Patriotic War. A total of 78 SC-497-class submarine chasers were provided by the United States; equipped with a 40mm Bofors gun and 12.7mm machine guns, these could achieve speeds of 18kn (33km/h) and had a range of 1,500nmi (2,778km) at 12kn (22km/h).

Torpedo boats were also used to provide fire support for amphibious landings by targeting harbour defences. The G5-class torpedo boat had a range of 220nmi (407km) and could achieve speeds of 58kn (107km/h); some 300 were built. The larger D3-class torpedo boat had a range of 350nmi (648km) at either 32kn (59km/h) for the first series or 45kn (83km/h) for the second series; 73 were built.

Sailors landed by submarines use dinghies to get to the shore, April 1942. The leading sailor has an SVT-40 semi-automatic rifle, with ammunition belts looped round his chest and waist; an RGD-33 anti-personnel fragmentation stick grenade is attached to his belt and he holds an ammunition container. The sailor to his left has a DP LMG. They are probably landing near Sevastopol as the use of surface warships would have been too dangerous. Only submarines and boats could bring out the last defenders of Sevastopol on 30 June 1942; others had to surrender or join the partisans. The commander of the 7th Naval Infantry Brigade, Colonel Evgeny Ivanovich Zhidilov, would be evacuated by submarine. (Sovfoto/Universal Images Group via Getty Images)

Towards the end of World War II, 30 LCI(L) landing craft were provided by the US Pacific Fleet; these could achieve speeds of 16kn (30km/h) and had a range of 500nmi (926km). Capable of embarking 188 troops and equipped with five 20mm guns plus machine guns, many were used to land Soviet forces on the Kuril Islands in the Western Pacific in August–September 1945.

OPERATIONS

The Arctic, 1941–42

In a bid to disrupt the German attempt to march on the important port of Murmansk from northern Norway, on 13 July 1941, 700 Northern Fleet sailors plus soldiers from the Red Army's 325th Rifle Division landed at Litsa Bay on the Murmansk coast of the Kola Peninsula. Determined to keep the route to Norway open, the Germans withdrew some units across the Litsa River, having failed to appreciate the ability of Soviet naval infantry to land on the coast and attack the road; the Axis attack towards Murmansk duly lost momentum.

In spring 1942, Soviet forces planned a landing at Cape Pikshuev on the Barents Sea, hoping to interdict the German line of withdrawal from the Litsa River in the face of frontal attacks mounted by the 152nd Rifle Division. On 28 April, the 12th Naval Infantry Brigade landed four battalions simultaneously at four locations on a 6km-long front, and by the end of the day a 7km×5km beachhead was established. With spring about to begin, cold-weather gear was not issued to the sailors; instead, the men had to make do with rain capes, cotton jackets and trousers, but these were not waterproof and would freeze. Despite two other battalions of the brigade also being landed, the Germans reacted quickly and took Hill 70 by Litsa Bay on 4 May. By then a snowstorm had descended, hampering the Soviet efforts; nearly 1,000 sailors would suffer weather-related injuries. When the bad weather abated on 10 May, German aircraft pounced on Soviet ships near Litsa Bay. With supplies running low, the 12th Naval Infantry Brigade was safely transported across the Litsa River on 13 May, having suffered 4,992 casualties.

The Baltic, 1941–43

By 7 August 1941, Axis troops of Heeresgruppe Nord had reached the Gulf of Finland, isolating Tallinn, the main fleet base on the Baltic Sea. The 1st Naval Infantry Brigade helped defend Tallinn. Three battalions of the brigade plus six battalions of sailors organized from base personnel were supported by coastal-defence artillery and naval gunfire. Altogether, some 14,000 sailors fought with the garrison of Tallinn, fully half of the defenders. Colonel I.G. Kostikov led the 3rd Naval Infantry Battalion plus a detachment of sailors in fighting near Pärnu on the approaches to the Tallinn naval base, but was surrounded; Kostikov died of his wounds, but most of his battalion made it back to the Soviet lines. Captain V. Sorokin's 3rd Naval Infantry Battalion mounted one company on trucks as a mobile reserve should the Germans penetrate the 7km line his battalion defended. The base could not hold out indefinitely, however. Almost the entire Baltic Fleet was at Tallinn and had to escape to Kronstadt. On 19 August, the final German attack on the city commenced. On 27 August, with a counter-attack by the defenders distracting the Germans, the Baltic Fleet set out for Kronstadt. Some 175 of 225 ships made it, with 18,000 men of the garrison on board, but at least 10,000 died, many of them civilians, on ships that were sunk by the Luftwaffe.

A cadet brigade of 1,748 sailors from educational establishments was formed at Leningrad (modern-day St Petersburg) on 1 July and sent to the Estonian border; on 5 September, after suffering defeat it would be disbanded, with most of its personnel joining those from the 1st Naval Infantry Brigade when they disembarked. By early September this brigade was sent to Krasnoye Selo to stop a German march on Leningrad. Lacking ammunition but with fixed bayonets, the sailors charged enemy positions immediately after disembarking; amid heavy casualties, all the battalion commanders were wounded. A single composite battalion was formed out of those able to continue fighting, but by early November this battalion and thus the brigade would be disbanded, too.

Soviet sailors guard the Barents Sea coast, 1942. From June 1941, the northern Arctic saw sustained Axis efforts to march on Murmansk, but the Soviet ability to land troops on the coast would distract the German forces and hinder their attempt to reach the port. Another German push was not contemplated seriously during 1942. Soviet forces would launch an attack on Petsamo in Finland during late 1944. (Keystone/Getty Images)

Heavily laden sailors, their rifles slung, move through Leningrad, 1942. The 2nd Naval Infantry Brigade, composed of five rifle battalions of sailors drawn from ships' crews, training detachments and coastal artillery units and with a tank battalion attached, held off Axis forces at Kotly during early September 1941, suffering 80 per cent casualties; on 30 August 1942, the brigade was redesignated the 48th Naval Rifle Brigade, still located at Oranienbaum. (Prisma by Dukas Presseagentur GmbH/Alamy Stock Photo)

By August, German forces threatened the approaches to Leningrad. In that city, the 2nd and 5th Naval Infantry brigades were formed, and assisted militia formations establish positions on the Luga Line and then near Oranienbaum on the Gulf of Finland. In September, both brigades held the Germans at Koporye, some 100km west of Leningrad. The position established at Oranienbaum would be maintained by the guns of Baltic Fleet ships based at Kronstadt; these defences distracted the Germans besieging Leningrad. On 2 September 1942, the 5th Naval Infantry Brigade was redesignated the 71st Naval Rifle Brigade.

The 3rd Naval Infantry Brigade, composed of four, later five, battalions, defended the sector north-east of Lake Ladoga near Leningrad; its troops would win fame for their sniping prowess. Initially, the brigade lacked its artillery and mortar battalions; these were added by early 1942. The brigade then deployed to the Arctic, though it saw little fighting there.

The 4th Naval Infantry Brigade fought against the Finns and would form four battalions; artillery assets included six 76mm and eight 45mm guns. Two

NAVAL INFANTRY, BALTIC, 1941

(1) Naval infantryman, 1941

This man's main weapon is the 7.62mm Mosin-Nagant M91/30 bolt-action rifle. Weighing 4kg, it had a non-detachable five-round magazine, loaded with rounds individually or by a clip. The effective range of the rifle was 500m. He wears the standard rifle-ammunition pouches on his waist belt, and belts of 7.62mm ammunition for the PM M1910 MMG around his waist and over each shoulder. He has wedged RGD-33 anti-personnel fragmentation stick grenades into his belt. The grenades shown here have a fragmentation sleeve; weighing 270g, this sleeve increased the RGD-33's blast radius from 10m to 15m. With the sleeve on, the RGD-33 was considered an offensive weapon; without it, it was a defensive weapon.

(2) *Stárshiy leytenánt*, naval infantry

The golden bands and star on this senior lieutenant's jacket sleeves indicate his rank. He is equipped with a 7.62mm Tokarev TT-33 semi-automatic pistol. The TT-33 supplemented the 7.62mm Nagant M1895 revolver in Soviet military service during the 1930s, but Nagant revolvers continued to be used during the Great Patriotic War and after. The TT-33's detachable magazine held eight rounds.

(3) DP gunner, naval infantry

This sailor is equipped with a 7.62mm DP LMG, the standard section support weapon. Fed by a 47-round circular pan attached to the top of the weapon, the DP had a rate of fire of only 550rd/min; the equivalent German weapon, the belt-fed 7.92mm MG 34 – essentially a GPMG as it could be fired from a bipod or a tripod – had a rate of fire of 800–900rd/min. This man also wears an RGD-33 grenade pouch on his waist belt, and an M34 cap bearing the designation of the Baltic Fleet on the cap band.

1

2

3

БАЛТИЙСКИЙ ФЛОТ

The naval rifle brigades, 1941–44

Naval-rifle brigades helped to launch the 1941/42 winter campaign against the German forces opposite Moscow. The 71st and 64th Naval Rifle brigades, formed by the Siberian and Urals Military districts mostly with sailors of the Pacific Fleet, were sent to Moscow, two of seven such brigades sent to defend the Soviet capital. The 64th Naval Rifle Brigade fought alongside the 24th Tank Brigade (20th Army) near Belyy Rast, 35km north of Moscow, against the 23. Infanterie-Division. The brigade held off stubborn German attacks on 7 December 1941, and then marched 130km as part of a two-week winter counter-attack. The brigade became the 82nd Rifle Division during June 1942.

The 71st Naval Rifle Brigade fought as part of the 1st Shock Army north-west of Moscow. On 5 January 1942 the brigade was redesignated the 2nd Guards Rifle Brigade. The 62nd Naval Rifle Brigade also fought in the 1st Shock Army, marching 180km on foot to do battle. By the following summer the 62nd Naval Rifle Brigade was sent to the Caucasus; at Krasnodar on 3 July 1943 the brigade was reorganized as the 257th Rifle Division. The 154th Naval Rifle Brigade fought alongside the 74th and 75th Naval Rifle brigades from the Central Asia Military District near Kholm. The 75th Naval Rifle Brigade would be renamed the 3rd Guards Rifle Brigade when it was pulled out of the front line in May 1942. The 66th and 154th Naval Rifle brigades fought on the Volga River during late 1942.

At the start of 1942, seven naval-rifle brigades – the 61st, 65th, 66th, 67th, 77th, 80th and 85th – fought with the Karelian Front against the Finns during the Continuation War (1941–44). Many surprise attacks would be carried out by scouts infiltrating the forests and using boats on the numerous water courses. Larger-scale attacks mounted by the 65th Naval Rifle Brigade on Finnish troops occupying defences among the marshes would be problematic because Soviet artillery could not be brought up. Finnish snipers in particular caused significant losses to the sailors, who disdained running from shelter to shelter.

The 68th, 76th, 78th, 79th, 81st and 83rd Naval Rifle brigades, formed by the North Caucasus Military District, were sent to the Southern Front. During March 1942, the 68th, 76th and 81st Naval Rifle brigades, operating with the 56th Army, landings on islands in Lake Ladoga ended with disastrous consequences; the Finns estimated that the Soviet forces lost 950 personnel during 26–27 July alone. As a consequence, the commander and commissar of the brigade's 2nd Battalion would be court-martialled and shot. Suitably 'encouraged', elements of Colonel I.G. Karkin's 3rd Battalion facing the Finns on the island of Rakhmansari fought to the last man during 4–8 September. On 19–20 September, elements of the 4th Naval Infantry Brigade, including the 1st Battalion, embarked on boats and sought to make a landing on the other side of the Neva River near Dubrovka in an effort to break the German encirclement of Leningrad. Although the battalion commander was killed, the naval infantry gained a foothold and other battalions of the brigade reinforced them, together with a Red Army rifle division. By mid-October, the 4th Naval Infantry Brigade's losses were such that only a single battalion could be mustered; by November, only a company was operational when the unit was withdrawn. By the end of 1941, reinforced to battalion strength, the 4th Naval Infantry Brigade was deployed on the southern shore of Lake Ladoga. After 400 men were sent to the 6th Naval Infantry Brigade, the 4th Naval Infantry Brigade was disbanded on 25 July 1942.

Formed from training-establishment personnel by late September 1941, the 6th Naval Infantry Brigade fought on the outskirts of Leningrad; by late October it was deployed outside the perimeter, and operated amid the swamps north of Novgorod alongside Red Army assets of the 54th Army. The brigade joined the 52nd Army's 138th Rifle Division on 16 May 1943.

Also formed in late September 1941, the 7th Naval Infantry Brigade took up positions at Pushkin, a critical defensive location near Leningrad. By the end of 1941 the brigade was transferred to Red Army control and was reorganized as the 72nd Rifle Division.

Separate battalions would also be raised, with some forming brigades in 1942. For example, the 260th Naval Infantry Brigade, formed on 20 July 1942, attacked German forces near Taganrog; some two-thirds of their personnel were casualties by July 1942, when the German summer offensive started. These brigades would mostly receive Red Army replacements. By June 1942, the 78th Naval Rifle Brigade, also manned mostly with Red Army personnel, had formed the 318th Rifle Division. The 79th Naval Rifle Brigade was sent to the Crimea to defend Sevastopol (see page 26). The 62nd Naval Rifle Brigade was sent from the North-West Front to the Taman Peninsula by September 1942; it would lose 5,838 men by late 1942, forming the 257th Rifle Division by June 1943. The 81st Naval Rifle Brigade was redesignated the 335th Infantry Regiment and landed at Eltigen in early November 1943, reinforcing the beachhead.

During September 1942, the 73rd Naval Rifle Brigade supported elements of the 2nd Shock Army in an unsuccessful bid to break the German encirclement of Leningrad. As German counter-attacks threatened to encircle the 2nd Shock Army, the brigade was ordered to keep an escape route open by capturing a hill near Tortolovo, a nearby town occupied by the invaders.

During the night of 27/28 September the 73rd Naval Rifle Brigade approached the hill through a marsh. A tank company and elements of the 265th Rifle Division assisted the attack the following morning. Soviet troops successfully occupied the hill as well as other heights nearby, repelling a series of German counter-attacks until 4 October and thus enabling the surrounded units to escape.

On 12 January 1943 the Soviet counter-offensive intended to free Leningrad from blockade commenced. The 55th Naval Rifle Brigade participated alongside troops of the 67th Army; though the attempt to break the encirclement of the city failed, a tank commander described the fighters as eagles not people, who rose to attack despite the risks. On 14 January 1944, the 2nd Shock Army, with the help of other naval-rifle brigades, pushed the German forces near Leningrad into Estonia.

During 1943–44, the other naval-rifle brigades still fighting would form Red Army rifle divisions or be disbanded; in such cases, the disbanded units' officers were sent back to the relevant fleet and the sailors joined Red Army units.

was composed of the 304th Separate Naval Infantry Battalion, which had defended Kotlin Island west of Leningrad in the Gulf of Finland since the start of the war, plus the SMG-equipped 571st Separate Naval Infantry Battalion and the 306th and 314th Separate Naval Infantry battalions. The brigade was sent to Kotlin Island and would be used for landing operations.

Odessa, 1941

The port of Odessa on the Black Sea was a key objective for Axis forces attacking from Romania during July 1941, and the Soviet defence of the city lasted from 5 August to 16 October. The 4th Romanian Army gradually encircled the city; the first main offensive against the port started on 16 August. Odessa was defended by two regiments of naval infantry (the 1st and 2nd) organized from base personnel. The Romanians did not break the main defensive line but they were able to target the harbour with long-range artillery fire. On 24 August a counter-attack mounted by the sailors repelled enemy forces seeking to target supply ships from Grigorievka on Lake Issyk Kul. Meanwhile, 6,000 sailors sent from Crimea to Odessa by late August formed six detachments to support the defence perimeter. By September, the 1st Naval Infantry Regiment became the 1330th Rifle Regiment of the Red Army's 421st Rifle Division. By mid-September, the 157th Rifle Division from the Kuban Peninsula joined the garrison at Odessa; soon after, the Romanians started another offensive.

A Soviet counter-attack to break the Axis forces' siege of Odessa included a landing by sea by sailors from Crimea. Starting at 0130hrs on 22 September, 1,920 men of the 3rd Naval Infantry Regiment landed at Grigorievka in support of the garrison's main attack. Soviet artillery fire stunned the Romanians and concealed the approach of launches and boats. The leading element of the regiment's 3rd Battalion was a company commanded by Junior Lieutenant I.D. Chorupa; he was closely followed by two others. They seized a Romanian artillery battery and turned its guns on the Axis forces. By 0500hrs, all three battalions had landed. At 0800hrs, two divisions from the Odessa garrison attacked; the Axis forces were thrown back, suffering 2,000 casualties, and were unable to bombard the city.

This only had a temporary effect, however, as the rapid march of German forces further east meant that Odessa remained isolated. The garrison was ordered to evade capture and by 16 October the Soviet evacuation was complete. Odessa had withstood 73 days under siege. The sailors redeployed to the Perekop Isthmus, the entrance to Crimea, joining the 1st and 4th battalions of the 7th Naval Infantry Brigade sent there, as part of the 51st Army.

Kerch, 1941–42

On 22 October 1941, having breached the Perekop Line, the Germans advanced on Kerch. The 9th Naval Infantry Brigade formed at Kerch held the approaches to the city with a battalion parcelling out companies among the forward Red Army rifle regiments. Out of 720 sailors, only 170 managed to escape when the Germans broke the line, capturing the city on 16 November. Though the brigade's artillery battalion only had a 45mm gun battery and 76mm gun battery, the other battalions delayed the Germans sufficiently to enable the evacuation of the city. No mortar battalion was formed either and the brigade possessed no radios. Altogether, 1,775 men of 4,200 from the 9th Naval Infantry Brigade would escape from Kerch by ship; 1,360 of them would be transported to Sevastopol and would be organized into two battalions to support the other brigades. The 9th Naval Infantry Brigade was re-formed from new recruits, personnel from Kerch naval base and wounded discharged from hospital. The brigade's 1st and 2nd battalions had only 300 men each because they sent contingents to form independent battalions for Kerch naval base and the Azov Flotilla. In April and May 1942, 4,278 sailors formed four infantry battalions, a mortar battalion and an artillery battalion. On 28 May most of the 9th Naval Infantry Brigade disembarked at Sevastopol (see pages 26–27) with eight 122mm guns, eight 76mm guns and 17 45mm guns, plus eight 82mm mortars and eight 120mm mortars.

In the closing days of 1941, the 51st Army's 83rd Naval Rifle Brigade and 224th Rifle Division spearheaded a Soviet landing on the Kerch Peninsula, a move intended to weaken the German forces besieging the port of Sevastopol. On 26 December, despite deteriorating weather conditions, the forward elements disembarked at some sites near Kerch and encountered only limited resistance. Soon, however, German aircraft caused significant losses among the larger Soviet ships and trawlers started to flounder because of poor weather; commanders found that they only had limited numbers of men on the beach. At Cape Zyuk, out of an intended 2,800 men only the 2nd Battalion of the 83rd Naval Rifle Brigade landed, and had to deal with the brunt of the German counter-attack on terrain with little cover; the weather conditions meant that most of the battalion's heavy weapons could not be unloaded. Only 1,378 men could be brought onto the beach; during 27–28 December they were attacked by two German battalions supported by bombers, and 300 sailors of the battalion were killed and 458 taken prisoner.

The 83rd Naval Rifle Brigade's most successful landing was made by 1,500 men at Khronya; two German battalions launched counter-attacks, but ships' guns provided fire support for the Soviet force as they endeavoured to keep hold of the beachhead. (On 3 January 1942, the 83rd Naval Rifle Brigade was redesignated as a naval-infantry brigade and continued to fight on the Kerch

Peninsula.) Units from the 44th Army that landed at Cape Kamysh-Burun, south of Kerch, found German defenders of the 46. Infanterie-Division close by; the Soviet forces successfully established beachheads, but only 2,175 of the intended 5,200 men got ashore because the larger ships ran aground.

Feodosiya, some 100km south-west of Kerch, was also targeted by the 44th Army; the city was stormed on 30 December 1941 by forces landed at the port, with 9th Naval Infantry Brigade detachments leading. The survivors of the 9th Naval Infantry Brigade – only 30 per cent of its original strength – joined the 83rd Naval Rifle Brigade when the operation ended. The Germans at Feodosiya had sent some units to Kerch, thereby weakening the Axis defences of Feodosiya; but the fact that Feodosiya was now occupied by Soviet forces persuaded the 46. Infanterie-Division to withdraw 120km from Kerch, through a snowstorm; Generalleutnant Hans von Sponeck, the German divisional commander, convinced he would be surrounded as a consequence of the Feodosiya landing, did not obey orders to crush the Soviet landing force at Kerch. By 1 January 1942, 23,000 Soviet troops had landed at Feodosiya. Although German forces sent from Sevastopol would quickly retake Feodosiya, Kerch would remain in Soviet hands until May 1942.

Prone naval infantry with SMGs in a featureless landscape. The first iteration of the 83rd Naval Rifle Brigade was formed near Krasnodar from ships' crews, naval reservists, cadets and volunteers; some sailors from Odessa joined them. The brigade had three battalions of 715 men each, an anti-tank battalion with 45mm guns, a mortar battalion with 82mm and 120mm mortars, an SMG company, a reconnaissance company, an ATR company, and an artillery battalion with eight 76mm guns. On 17 December 1941 the brigade commenced its first combat mission, to land on the Kerch Peninsula. (Nik Cornish at www.stavka.org.uk)

Sevastopol, 1941–42

The breaching of the Perekop Line also made Sevastopol a target for the Germans. The 2nd and 3rd Naval Infantry regiments and the 7th Naval Infantry Brigade were sent to Sevastopol to serve alongside five battalions formed from a training detachment, two battalions raised from cadets from the Lenin Komsomol Sevastopol Naval School of Coastal Defence, a battalion of sailors from the Danube Flotilla and, from 30 October, the 8th Naval Infantry Brigade from Novorossiysk: a total of 22,300 sailors.

On 2 November, the 5th Battalion of the 7th Naval Infantry Brigade, marching by road to Sevastopol, suffered heavy casualties when it was attacked by elements of the 50. Infanterie-Division. The battalion commander was killed and only 300 sailors managed to entrench on a hill nearby. By the end of the day, 50 men with the commissar tried to break out of the encirclement; only 37 made it to Sevastopol. On 5 November, the 7th Naval Infantry Brigade successfully sent the 1st and 2nd battalions to defences around Sevastopol; the 3rd and 4th battalions would be sent by sea. The 7th Naval Infantry Brigade fought at Mekenzi Farm until 17 November, when it was withdrawn after suffering heavy losses. When the Germans launched a second attack on Sevastopol in December, the brigade was used to counter-attack Mount Gasfort.

On 7 November a unit of cadets, the 18th Naval Infantry Battalion, fought German armour at Duvankoy. Commissar Nikolay Filchenkov tied grenades to his body and flung himself under a German tank; four other sailors – Ivan Krasnoselsky, Daniil Odintsov, Yuri Parshin and Vasily Tsybulko – would also be awarded the title Hero of the Soviet Union for their efforts to defeat the Panzers. (In total, 200 sailors of the naval brigades would be awarded the title Hero of the Soviet Union during the Great Patriotic War.)

In the closing weeks of 1941, 32 battalions of sailors defended Sevastopol; the 79th Naval Rifle Brigade was deployed in defence of the city. Naval personnel also constituted whole battalions of many Red Army units engaged in the defence. The 345th and 388th Rifle divisions joined the Soviet garrison by mid-December 1941. The 79th Naval Rifle Brigade counter-attacked at Sevastopol on 23 December 1941, pushing the Germans off Hills 104.5 and 192; its personnel reached the Belbek valley, allowing the Red Army's 287th Rifle Regiment to break out of the encirclement. By the end of 1941, however, the Germans decided instead to blockade Sevastopol as their attacks had failed.

Soviet sailors counter-attack near Sevastopol. The 8th Naval Infantry Brigade had deployed to Balaklava to stall a German attempt to encircle the city. On 2 November 1941 the brigade inflicted 428 casualties on the enemy, forcing a delay for a week to enable the Germans to bring up further formations. This gave the Soviet Navy time to transport 20,000 soldiers to Sevastopol to help the sailors and by mid-November the garrison numbered some 52,000 men. (Sovfoto/Universal Images Group via Getty Images)

By mid-January 1942, the 8th Naval Infantry Brigade and the 2nd Naval Infantry Regiment had been disbanded, with their personnel sent to the 7th Naval Infantry Brigade and the 79th Naval Rifle Brigade. In mid-1942 the Germans attacked Sevastopol again, starting on 7 June. By then, the 79th Naval Rifle Brigade was composed of three rifle battalions, a mortar battalion with eight 82mm mortars and a second with eight 120mm mortars, an artillery battalion with four 122mm and eight 76mm guns and an anti-tank battalion with six 45mm guns, plus four other companies (machine-gun, ATR, reconnaissance and sapper). Occupying bunkers and trenches and protected by mines and barbed wire, each rifle battalion had three rifle companies, a machine-gun company and an 82mm mortar company. Following five days of artillery preparation, the Germans attacked, intent on capturing Mekenzi Farm. The 79th Naval Rifle Brigade fought a stable defensive battle; despite the Germans committing armour, they were able to gain only 300–400m of ground per day. A contingent of 400 men of the 79th Naval Rifle Brigade defended the Balaklava highway; a German tank unit approaching the brigade lost 20 tanks, but it was a success won at the cost of 75 per cent casualties among the sailors.

By the end of June 1942, the Germans had gained positions overlooking the city despite ferocious resistance typified by the actions of Alexander K. Chikarenko, who decided on 25 June to blow himself up along with 200 Germans by detonating a warehouse of ammunition located at the Sukharnaya gully ammunition depot. On 27 June the last Soviet surface ship departed Sevastopol. Street fighting started on 30 June. The 7th and 9th Naval Infantry brigades would be destroyed during the final German assault on the city.

Naval infantrymen in greatcoats, led by NCOs, move through Sevastopol, April 1942; note the manner in which the leading man's PPSh-41 SMG is slung. During August and September 1941 the 7th Naval Infantry Brigade formed at barracks around Sevastopol. Each of its five battalions had three rifle companies, a machine-gun company and an artillery battery of 76mm guns. When two battalions were sent to the Perekop Isthmus, two more were formed in their place. The brigade also had a mortar battalion. (Sovfoto/ Universal Images Group via Getty Images)

Novorossiysk, 1942–43

When the Germans moved over to the offensive in the summer of 1942, the danger of a breakthrough to the Caucasus was apparent. From August, the 83rd Naval Infantry Brigade deployed from coastal-defence duty to deal with the Axis armoured spearheads; and from May 1942, after its withdrawal from the Kerch Peninsula, the brigade received men who had fought with the 64th, 68th, 76th and 81st Naval Rifle brigades as well as other personnel from ships' crews. They formed at Novorossiysk and trained throughout June and July.

On 27 August the 1st Naval Infantry Brigade (renamed the 255th Naval Infantry Brigade on 25 September) joined them. Commanded by Lieutenant Colonel Dmitry Vasilyevich Gordeev, this brigade was composed of the 14th, 142nd and 322nd Separate Naval Infantry battalions, formed from personnel of the Caspian and Azov Sea flotillas. Gordeev's brigade fought its way out of encirclement through the Caucasus to Novorossiysk. Alongside the 83rd Naval Infantry Brigade, the 1st Naval Infantry Brigade fought near Novorossiysk as part of the 47th Army as part of Soviet efforts to stall the German approach during mid-August; the 81st Naval Rifle Brigade and the 137th Naval Infantry Regiment were also involved in the defence of the city. A Soviet defensive line was formed with the support of the 144th Separate Naval Infantry Battalion.

On 3 September the German assault on Novorossiysk commenced. The cement works was defended by the 83rd Naval Infantry Brigade's 1st Battalion, led by the regiment's chief-of-staff, Senior Lieutenant Ivan Vasilyevich Zhernovoy. After a series of street battles, the survivors of the brigade then escaped encirclement by breaking out to Stanichki, a suburb of Novorossiysk, being evacuated from a nearby beach by boat on 10 September. The 16th, 144th and 305th Separate Naval Infantry battalions also fought alongside the brigade; the 83rd Naval Infantry Brigade was reconstituted with these battalions as its original battalions could no longer function properly. Despite these independent battalions' recent formation, their sailors had shown signs of combat proficiency.

On 25 September, the reconstituted 83rd Naval Infantry Brigade (16th, 144th and 305th Separate Naval Infantry battalions) successfully completed

Sailors wearing traditional reefer jackets and Soviet Navy caps are depicted in an urban environment, possibly Novorossiysk, during late 1943. The man changing a magazine in the foreground has a PPS-43 SMG, while the two men behind him have the older PPSh-41 SMG. The 83rd Naval Infantry Brigade was almost annihilated when the German attack in spring 1942 began; the survivors were sent to Novorossiysk and the Taman Peninsula. By late 1943 the brigade had a 215-strong SMG battalion, a 120mm mortar battalion, a 76mm artillery battalion and a 45mm anti-tank battalion supporting its rifle battalions. They would fight on the streets at Novorossiysk by late 1943. (Courtesy of the Central Museum of the Armed Forces, Moscow via Stavka)

its first attack despite lacking a full complement of artillery. On 1 October the brigade was posted to Tuapse to fight off German attempts to break through the Caucasus, in conjunction with the 68th and 76th Naval Rifle brigades, the 137th and 145th Naval Infantry regiments (formed from wounded sailors from Sevastopol) and the 323rd Separate Naval Infantry Battalion.

Stanichki, February 1943

By early 1943 the Germans had started to withdraw from the Caucasus. On 1 February, the Soviet 47th Army started its attack on Novorossiysk. To support the ground forces a landing by sea was planned for 4 February. Gordeev (by now a colonel) commanded the landing force; he planned a landing by two naval-infantry brigades at Yuzhnaya Ozereyka to seize Novorossiysk. The Azov Battalion, commanded by Major Tsesar Lvovich Kunikov, would land at Stanichki, a suburb of Novorossiysk, to distract the enemy.

At Ozereyka the Soviet bombardment targeting the defences was unsuccessful because of poor fire correction. At 0245hrs on 4 February the bombardment stopped, alerting the Axis defenders that something was about to happen. Only at 0335hrs did the first boats appear, however, having been delayed by poor weather. They were quickly targeted by German artillery batteries supporting the Romanian defenders. Although 1,427 men made it to the beach, the first-echelon commander was killed by a direct hit on the cutter *SKA-051*. Tugs bringing floating pontoons were also hit. Elements of all three rifle battalions of the 255th Naval Infantry Brigade were soon stranded on the beach without a single radio between them. The brigade commander and his staff had not disembarked. Gunboats and trawlers following the initial landing force had to turn away because of enemy fire. Despite these difficulties, however, by attacking up a gully the Soviet forces got off the beach, hitting the Romanians from an unexpected quarter. The Axis defenders abandoned their positions, but by the end of the day the Germans had brought up an infantry battalion with tank support. The naval infantry had pushed further on, allowing the Romanians to re-occupy the beach positions. While 150 naval infantry were able to withdraw to Stanichki, only 25 men would be evacuated by boat.

On 4 February, a minesweeper commenced firing Katyusha rockets on the Axis defences at Stanichki. The Soviet assault unit that landed at Stanichki was composed of 250 volunteers equipped with SMGs, ATRs, mortars and machine guns. The detachment had received training on Cape Tonkiy near Gelendzhik on the Black Sea, including instruction on climbing cliffs and using captured German equipment. Fighting was fierce and often at close quarters. Trawlers destined for Ozereyka were sent to Stanichki, bringing the total number of Soviet troops landed to 800. The beachhead was 4km wide with a depth of 2.5km.

At dawn on 4 February the Germans launched strong counter-attacks on Stanichki, countered by fire from Soviet coastal artillery and supporting gun batteries. Late on 6 February, units of the 255th Naval Infantry Brigade and the 165th Rifle Brigade were disembarked. By 17 February, 17,000 men had landed, widening the beachhead. A total of four rifle brigades and some partisan detachments would follow by 18 February and the Red Army's 176th Rifle Division from 22 February. Soviet supplies and reinforcements had to be brought in by sea during the hours of darkness, however, as the Germans could observe the beachhead from nearby heights.

By the end of May, 40,000 Soviet personnel would be opposed by twice as many Axis troops, sent from other locations. Each company of the 83rd Naval Infantry Brigade had up to 20 Communist Party members and 25 Komsomol members. Of Kunikov's Azov Battalion, 127 sailors would be decorated for valour as would 1,318 sailors from the 83rd Naval Infantry Brigade. The battle to maintain the Soviet beachhead, known as Malaya Zemlya, would last for 218 days, but Novorossiysk was not yet liberated.

The Novorossiysk–Taman Operation

On 10 September 1943, the Soviet bid to liberate the Taman Peninsula from the German 17. Armee began. The Germans had decided to withdraw from the peninsula following their defeat at Kursk and the subsequent Soviet Donbass offensive; the Novorossiysk–Taman Operation had the aim of stopping them from getting away. All told, some 317,400 men equipped with 4,435 artillery pieces and mortars and supported by 314 tanks and self-propelled guns faced about 400,000 Axis troops equipped with 2,800 artillery pieces and mortars and backed by 100 tanks and self-propelled guns.

The Soviet attack on Novorossiysk was launched from Malaya Zemlya, with a landing by boat taking place at the port. Additionally, Red Army units near Tuapse would march on the city from the south-east. The Soviet boats would need to get past 40 Axis gun batteries located along the shoreline. The landing support detachment, composed of 32 torpedo boats, had the task of breaking the barriers at the entrance to the port. The disembarkation force had 120 combat and support boats and 28 motor launches to land sailors. The Axis beach defences would be targeted by the torpedo boats while the artillery tackled the other Axis defences. The assault force was composed of the 255th Naval Infantry Brigade and the 393rd Separate Naval Infantry Battalion – 4,000 sailors – plus an NKVD regiment and the Red Army's 1339th Rifle Regiment: 6,480 men in total. The 393rd Separate Naval Infantry Battalion had recently been formed from Novorossiysk personnel and was named after Major Kunikov.

Late on 9 September, the 255th Naval Infantry Brigade embarked on boats at Gelendzhik. They had trained on positions constructed to replicate the German defences, including practising embarking on boats at night in rough weather. The infantry practised beach landings and sappers particularly focused on demolishing beach obstructions; commissars concentrated on bolstering the sailors' morale. Those personnel new to the naval infantry had past campaigns described to them, while veterans of previous amphibious landings explained the means used to gain a beachhead.

At 0244hrs on 10 September, torpedo boats launched 24 torpedoes at targets on the pier and beach front and demolished 19 Axis bunkers. At 0256hrs, once the net barrier was breached, torpedo boats sped to the harbour and launched torpedoes at other beach defences. From 0300hrs, launches started landing elements of the 393rd Separate Naval Infantry Battalion; some boats' captains could not see properly because of poor weather and would land the battalion on a front of 6km, not 1.2km as planned. All told, 800 men with ten mortars, 19 MMGs and 40 ATRs were landed on the northern bay area in the teeth of Axis artillery and machine-gun fire. Although the Soviet watercraft strove to dodge the detonations as they headed to shore, 13 boats would be sunk on the day of the landing. Meanwhile, 1,083 men of the 1339th Rifle Regiment landed at Importnaya Pier and the 255th Naval Infantry Brigade's first-echelon contingent landed at the Kabotazhnaya Pier. The water level at the landing site was shallow and men had to land by motor boat. At least four hours be needed to get the men on to the beach.

The first units ashore of the 255th Naval Infantry Brigade did not secure the landing ground on the north-western coast, however, having instead decided to get off the beach. These initial units became isolated from each other and the second-echelon units found that they were unable to land on the intended beach sector, instead being compelled to land where the third landing detachment was supposed to come ashore. Most units of the 255th Naval Infantry Brigade would be forced to withdraw to Stanichki.

The 1339th Rifle Regiment's landing quickly developed into a fierce battle by the fortified power plant at Importnaya Pier. Once this was occupied, the 318th Rifle Division decided to land its 1337th Rifle Regiment during the early hours of 12 September. The Red Army men linked up with the 393rd

The war against Japan, 1945

Naval infantry assisted the Red Army in the seizure of Manchuria following the Soviet Union's declaration of war on Japan on 9 August 1945. The Soviet Union attacked the poorly equipped Japanese forces garrisoning Manchuria from multiple directions; following the Soviet breakthrough, Japanese forces started to withdraw to the port of Seishin (modern-day Chongjin, North Korea), and so a Soviet landing at the port was organized to stop them escaping. The Soviet forces involved – 5,971 men, embarked on landing ships, torpedo boats, coast-guard ships and submarine chasers – included the 13th Naval Infantry Brigade, the 355th Separate Naval Infantry Battalion and one company from the 62nd Separate Naval Infantry Battalion. Soviet air support was provided by 188 bombers and 73 fighters.

Colonel A.Z. Denisin, the chief of intelligence at Pacific Fleet Headquarters, was the commander of the 181-strong assault force, composed of the 140th Reconnaissance Detachment plus two companies, one each from the 62nd and 355th Separate Naval Infantry battalions. At 0700hrs on 13 August they departed Novik Bay on torpedo boats. At 1338hrs the torpedo boats arrived at Seishin and landed the scouts and the 335th Separate Naval Infantry Battalion by the berths. The Japanese counter-attacked and isolated the assault force by occupying the beach. The 80-strong machine-gun company from the 62nd Separate Naval Infantry Battalion was sent to assist, but could not establish communications with the assault detachment. At 0455hrs on 14 August, two further companies of the 355th Separate Naval Infantry Battalion commanded by Major M.P. Barabalko landed near the docks; one company occupied the railway station and joined up with Denisin. The Japanese could quickly bring greater numbers to Seishin, however, and the situation for the naval infantry looked bleak. Denisin withdrew to the pier and occupied a narrow strip of shoreline only 300–400m wide.

Having set out at 0500rs on 14 August, the main Soviet force of 23 ships carrying the 13th Naval Infantry Brigade landed at Seishin on 15 August in the teeth of Japanese artillery fire. On 16 August the brigade was reinforced with two artillery battalions, seven T-26 light tanks, three self-propelled guns and 100 trucks brought to the piers. By the end of that day, Soviet forces had established control of the port; some 3,000 Japanese defenders were

E **NAVAL INFANTRY, PACIFIC FLEET, 1945**

(1) Stárshiy serzhánt, naval infantry
This scout wears an M1943 tunic; he is a member of the Pacific Fleet, as indicated on his cap and shoulder boards, the latter also displaying the thick band indicating his rank of senior sergeant. His medals include the Order of the Patriotic War First Class (right breast), the Medal for Battle Merit (the circle on his left breast) and the Order of Glory, 2nd Class (the star). His 'amoeba'-camouflage trousers are of a style first produced in the late 1930s and issued to snipers and reconnaissance units. He wears an ammunition pouch for his 7.62mm PPS-43 SMG as well as an SVT-40 bayonet and an RGD-33 anti-personnel fragmentation stick grenade.

(2) DP gunner, naval infantry
Having discarded his tunic, this man wears his *telnyashka* and khaki trousers; traditionally, if an infantryman wore only the undershirt, it meant that he was prepared to fight to the death. He has a magazine pouch carrying 47-round circular pans for his 7.62mm DP LMG slung over his left shoulder. The RPG-43 anti-tank hand grenade he carries was a high-explosive anti-tank (HEAT) grenade using a shaped-charge warhead; weighing 1.35kg, it had 612g of high explosive. When the RPG-43 was thrown, a cylindrical metal cone would be released from the back of the grenade and held by lines of fabric so the flight was stabilized. The grenade had to hit armour at an angle near to perpendicular for the charge to work, however, and strike it sufficiently hard to detonate the fuze.

(3) Yefréytor, naval infantry
This machine-gunner, a *yefréytor* (lance corporal) of the Pacific Fleet, is maintaining his 7.62mm SG-43 MMG during a lull in the fighting. He has a pistol holster on his belt. The air-cooled SG-43 was the successor to the 7.62mm PM M1910 MMG and was likewise mounted on a wheeled carriage with gun shield; ammunition was fed from 200- or 250-round belts and the cyclic rate was 500–700rd/min.

either killed or taken prisoner. In recognition of their role in the operation, the 13th Naval Infantry Brigade and the 355th Separate Naval Infantry Battalion were named Guards units.

The 77th Separate Naval Infantry Battalion (13th Naval Infantry Brigade) then landed at the port of Odentsin (modern-day Odaejin, North Korea) on 18 August. On 20 August the port of Genzan (modern-day Wŏnsan, North Korea) was the target of a landing by a 1,847-strong force composed of troops from the 13th Naval Infantry Brigade plus the 140th Reconnaissance Detachment. The Japanese did not want to fight or surrender, but negotiations by 22 August obtained a Japanese capitulation by 6,000 men.

On 16 August, having travelled through stormy weather and fog, Soviet Navy ships landed the 365th Separate Naval Infantry Battalion and the 113th Rifle Brigade at Tōro (modern-day Shakhtyorsk, Russia) on south Sakhalin, the troops moving directly onto the pier and nearby sand bars. On 17 August they linked up with a machine-gun company that landed at the port of Esutoru (modern-day Uglegorsk, Russia). On 25 August a 1,600-strong composite brigade, comprising three battalions, landed at Otomari (modern-day Korsakov, Russia). The force did not encounter any organized resistance and the Japanese forces on the island surrendered.

Defended by 60,000 Japanese soldiers with 77 tanks, the Soviet invasion of the Kuril Islands would be another matter. Late on 16 August, a composite naval-infantry battalion boarded ships for Shumshu, the largest of the Kuril Islands in the Sea of Okhotsk, landing at 0430hrs on 18 August. A rifle regiment from the Red Army's 101st Rifle Division landed soon after the naval infantry, followed by a second regiment; the Soviet landing force soon numbered 8,300 men in total, facing 8,500 Japanese defenders. The beach was quickly occupied and the naval infantry and soldiers pushed forward; Japanese strongpoints and entrenchments had to be stormed by the Soviet troops to guarantee additional landing sites, but emplaced Japanese artillery would continue to disrupt the landings of additional Soviet echelons, with seven landing craft being sunk during the day. The naval infantry already ashore were initially unable to communicate effectively with headquarters elements aboard the ships because 21 of the 22 available radios were waterlogged and out of action. In addition, the Soviet troops had only four 45mm guns on the beach.

Hills 165 and 171 on the north-eastern part of the island were occupied by the Soviet forces by 0920hrs, with artillery barrages requested via the only working radio aiding the attack. A rapid Japanese counter-attack soon took the heights again, however. By 1400hrs the Japanese had committed 18 tanks with two battalions of infantry to a counter-attack near Hill 171; the Soviet forces' four 45mm guns and ATRs held them off. Near Hill 165 the naval infantry were forced to rely on anti-tank grenades to defend against 20 Japanese tanks. Desperate men committed selfless acts to blow up the enemy tanks and many died doing so. By the end of the day the Soviet forces had occupied the heights, meaning the landing of additional supplies could begin. At 1800hrs on 19 August the Japanese commander proposed a truce and the fighting halted. On 22 August the 50,000 Japanese began surrendering, and by 1 September all of the Kuril Islands were occupied by Soviet forces. On Shumshu the Soviets suffered 1,567 casualties, the Japanese 1,018.

NAVAL INFANTRY IN THE COLD WAR

DRAWDOWN AND REBIRTH

At the end of the Great Patriotic War, the military priority for Stalin's regime was the development of an operational nuclear weapon to counter the threat posed by the United States' nuclear capability. Until then, large ground forces were still deemed necessary to defend the Soviet satellite states of Eastern Europe from attempts by the United States and NATO to foment political unrest to weaken communist power. In a future conflict, the Soviet Navy's ships would assist the Soviet Army by delaying the enemy. This subordinate role for the Soviet Navy entailed cutbacks in naval expenditure at a time when the country had to be rebuilt after the ravages of the recent global conflict.

Although some Soviet Navy fleets organized naval-infantry formations after the end of the Great Patriotic War, by 1946 only six naval-infantry brigades and ten separate battalions remained operational. By September 1945, the Pacific Fleet had re-established the 15th Naval Infantry Brigade, but it included only the 98th Separate Naval Infantry Battalion by 1946. On 19 January 1946, the 14th Naval Infantry Brigade was established on the Kamchatka Peninsula with the 79th 80th, 81st and 82nd Separate Naval Infantry battalions plus an SMG battalion. By September 1947, the 13th Naval Infantry Brigade had been disbanded, but the 120th Naval Infantry Brigade (354th, 609th and 610th Separate Naval Infantry battalions) was formed on Russky Island in the Pacific Fleet's area of operations.

By 1948, the naval infantry was reorganized, with some units reassigned to the coastal-defence forces. Many units were disbanded by 1955, with the 355th, 365th, 364th and 98th Separate Naval Infantry battalions and the 120th Naval Infantry Brigade ceasing to exist. By July 1956, the 14th Naval Infantry Brigade and the only battalion on the Baltic, the 94th Separate Naval Infantry Battalion, were also disbanded.

The commander-in-chief of the Soviet Navy, Admiral Nikolay Gerasimovich Kuznetsov, was dismissed in February 1956 because he tried to argue for a strong fleet. In the 1950s, the continued focus on developing a Soviet strategic nuclear capability led to the marginalization of the Soviet Navy until its submarines could carry long-range nuclear weapons in the 1960s. In this new climate, the armed forces shed manpower; amphibious operations and the development of associated technologies were seen by many policymakers as impractical because they were vulnerable to enemy missile systems. (Universal History Archive/Universal Images Group via Getty Images)

Admiral Sergey Georgyevich Gorshkov, the commander-in-chief of the Soviet Navy during 1956–85, was crucial to the rebirth of the Soviet naval infantry in the 1960s and its expansion in the 1970s. The influence of the expanding Soviet Navy on his watch would be demonstrated in 1957, when the Nasser regime in Egypt requested Soviet assistance; major Soviet Navy assets were deployed in the region.

On 14 July 1958, the United States military showed it could rapidly deploy amphibious forces when they landed on the Lebanese coast to deter the Soviet Union from sending military help to rebel forces in Lebanon. The Cuban Missile Crisis of 16–29 October 1962 saw the US Navy being able to blockade the Caribbean to Soviet Navy ships because the Soviet Union did not possess an ocean-going fleet. While such a fleet could not be constructed straightaway, the Soviet Union could exert itself closer to home. Keen to project Soviet power abroad at a time when NATO's Polaris submarines and carrier groups deployed to the Eastern Mediterranean and the Norwegian Sea, Soviet strategists argued that in times of heightened international tensions, the Soviet Navy would need to deploy further forward – beyond the 200–300nmi (370–556km) zone it hitherto defended – in order to stop nuclear weapons targeting the Soviet Union. To seize entrances to sea lanes of communication and enable such a deployment, a specialized force of naval infantry was needed. The possession of such an asset would also permit power projection, enabling the Soviet Union to influence the course of events during political crises aboard.

By the mid-1960s this shift of emphasis was evident; Gorshkov spoke of strategic tasks such as destroying enemy surface shipping or coastal targets around the world. By 1968, the interdiction of sea lanes of communication would be stated as the Soviet Navy's purpose. Gorshkov's involvement was critical to the drafting of a fleet mission statement that included amphibious landing forces. By 1964 the naval infantry had been re-established, initially numbering some 2,000–3,000 personnel but rising to 15,000 by 1971.

By the 1970s, Soviet Navy assets were spending more time in the Mediterranean Sea than their US Navy counterparts, including a substantial increase in the number of Soviet Navy port visits – some 955 in 1971–73. By 1973 each fleet would have a brigade-strength naval-infantry unit capable of conducting amphibious landings, holding beachheads and defending bases. During peacetime, possessing a force of naval infantry aboard amphibious ships gave Soviet strategic planners a wider range of options while pursuing the Soviet Union's stated foreign-policy aims, though the lack of amphibious support ships and dedicated naval aircraft limited the influence the naval infantry could have during the 1970s.

EXPANSION OF THE NAVAL INFANTRY

On 7 June 1963, the 336th Separate Guards Marine Regiment of the Baltic Fleet was formed from the Soviet Army's 336th Guards Motor Rifle Regiment (120th Guards Motor Rifle Division) and headquartered at Baltiysk, Kaliningrad. Also in 1963, the 390th Separate Marine Regiment of the Pacific Fleet was created from the Soviet Army's 390th Motor Rifle Regiment (56th Motor Rifle Division) and headquartered at Slavyanka on the Sea of Japan.

In the spring of 1966, the 1st Battalion of the 336th Separate Guards Marine Regiment, supplemented with Soviet Army personnel from the 135th Motor Rifle Regiment (295th Motor Rifle Division), formed

the 309th Separate Marine Battalion, Black Sea Fleet, and deployed to Sevastopol. On 14 May that year, the Soviet Army's 61st Motor Rifle Regiment (131st Motor Rifle Division, Leningrad Military District) became the 61st Separate Marine Regiment of the Northern Fleet and was headquartered at Pechenga on the Barents Sea.

During 1967, one rifle company from the 61st Separate Marine Regiment and another from the 336th Separate Guards Marine Regiment deployed to the Pacific to create the 106th Marine Regiment. On 15 December that year, the 810th Separate Marine Regiment of the Black Sea Fleet was formed at Sevastopol from the 309th Separate Marine Battalion plus a company of amphibious tanks from the 61st Separate Marine Regiment. The third battalion was only a cadre, though during exercises this third battalion would be mobilized.

By 1967 the decision was made to establish a marine division in the Soviet Navy. In the latter part of 1968 the 55th Marine Division was officially formed, based on the 106th, 165th and 390th Marine regiments plus a tank regiment, the 150th, alongside battalion-sized support units; personnel strength was 7,000 all ranks. By 1970, the division's 263rd Separate Reconnaissance Battalion plus one battalion from the 165th Marine Regiment had completed airborne training with parachutes. By the early 1980s the division had also gained artillery and air-defence regiments.

The strategic role of the naval infantry expanded through the 1970s to include the ability to seize important sea lanes such as the Baltic Straits. NATO forces began to deploy carrier groups and nuclear-armed submarines further forward and Soviet planners believed that the deployment of larger marine brigades would deter them by possessing a capability to capture straits and narrows. On 20 November 1979 the 810th Separate Marine Brigade, totalling 2,300 men, was formed from the regiment of that number, fielding the 880th, 882nd and 885th Marine battalions plus the 881st Separate Airborne Battalion, 888th Reconnaissance Battalion, 113th Tank Battalion, 1613th Self-Propelled Artillery Battalion, 1616th MRL battalion, 1619th Air Defence Battalion, 1622nd Anti-Tank Battalion; an engineer landing company, a communications company, a support company and a map platoon completed the organization.

The 336th Separate Guards Marine Regiment was also redesignated a brigade on 20 November 1979. Its component units included the 877th,

878th and 884th Marine battalions and the 879th Marine Airborne Battalion, plus the 112th Tank Battalion, the 887th Reconnaissance Battalion and the usual mix of supporting elements.

On 15 May 1980, the 61st Separate Marine Regiment became a brigade with the same structure as the 810th Separate Marine Brigade. By 1989 the brigade was composed of the 874th, 875th and 883rd Separate Marine battalions plus the 876th Marine Airborne Battalion, as well as the 886th Reconnaissance Battalion and the usual mix of supporting elements.

The 175th Separate Marine Brigade of the Northern Fleet was formed at the end of 1981. To start with it was a cadre brigade and did not exceed 200 personnel. It was issued the same equipment as the 61st Separate Marine Brigade and could be expanded if necessary.

ORGANIZATION

In 1966, the 309th Separate Marine Battalion had three rifle companies, one tank company, a mortar platoon, an armoured personnel carrier (APC) platoon, a reconnaissance platoon, an engineer landing platoon, a communications platoon and a truck platoon.

In the early 1970s, each 400-man infantry battalion (25 BTR-60PB APCs) had three rifle companies, supported by a mortar platoon (50 men, six 82mm mortars), an anti-tank platoon (three tripod-mounted 73mm SPG-9 Kopyo anti-tank guns), a communications section and a medical half-section plus a small supply and maintenance platoon. Each rifle company (six officers, 106 men) had a headquarters section, three 30-man platoons and a general-purpose machine gun (GPMG) section. As well as its integral 82mm mortar platoon, the rifle battalion could call upon brigade-level assets such as 120mm mortars and multiple rocket launchers (MRLs).

In 1967, the 810th Separate Marine Regiment included an air-defence battery equipped with 23mm ZSU-23-4 Shilka self-propelled anti-aircraft guns (SPAAGs) and 9K31 Strela-1 surface-to-air missiles (SAMs), an MRL battery with BM-14-17 rocket launchers mounted on GAZ-63A 4×4 trucks, a self-propelled artillery battery with SU-100 tank destroyers, an anti-tank battery with 9M14 Malyutka anti-tank guided missiles (ATGMs) mounted on BRDM-2 amphibious armoured scout cars, an engineer landing company, a signals company, a reconnaissance platoon and a supply company. The brigades' small size limited the naval infantry to conducting small-scale commando-type raids or spoiling attacks; without support from ground forces, no large independent amphibious operations could be contemplated.

In 1979, the 810th Separate Marine Brigade's tank battalion had three companies with 13 T-55M main battle tanks (MBTs) each plus one with 13 PT-76 amphibious light tanks. The brigade's MRL battalion had a battery of 122mm BM-21 Grad MRLs; the air-defence battery fielded 23mm ZSU-23-4 Shilka SPAAGs and 9K35 Strela-10 SAMs. By 1989, the brigade had added a self-propelled artillery battalion to its force structure with 18 122mm 2S1 self-propelled howitzers and 24 120mm 2S9 rifled howitzers for airborne use, alongside the 9P138 Grad 1 MRLs.

By the mid-1980s, each naval infantry brigade (2,059 all ranks) had three infantry battalions, each with three rifle companies, plus a tank battalion equipped with PT-76s and T-54/55s. Each infantry battalion had 34 BTR-60PB APCs: each rifle company had ten, battalion headquarters had one, and the anti-tank platoon had three, plus three man-portable 9M14 Malyutka

Pictured in April 1990, the second helicopter carrier of the Moskva class, *Leningrad*, was commissioned in 1968. Designed for anti-submarine warfare but capable of carrying a battalion of naval infantry, these ships could be used to provide a Soviet military presence in places where a political crisis was brewing. (U.S. Department of Defense/Wikimedia/Public Domain)

ATGMs and three 73mm SPG-9 Kopyo anti-tank guns. The battalion's mortar platoon had three 82mm or 120mm mortars transported on lorries. In terms of small arms, each rifle company had nine 7.62mm RPK LMGs, nine RPG-7 rocket-propelled grenade launchers, three 9K32M Strela-2M SAMs and three 7.62mm SVD marksman rifles. The brigade's tank battalion had three companies, each with three platoons of four tanks plus a tank for the company commander; a mix of PT-76 amphibious light tanks and T-55 MBTs were used. These assets were supported by an engineer company to clear mines and obstacles, a reconnaissance company, an anti-tank battery with six BRDM-2 amphibious armoured scout cars mounting the 9M14 Malyutka ATGM system, an MRL battery equipped with 122mm BM-21 Grad MRLs, an air-defence battery and a chemical-defence company. The reconnaissance company had three PT-76s and nine BRDM-2s.

EVOLVING DOCTRINE

While the collapse of European global empires after 1945 presented the Soviet Union with opportunities for influence with newly created countries – lucrative commercial deals could be influenced by military power-projection capabilities – the importance of the European land mass continued to dominate Soviet strategic thought. The Northern Fleet had the Soviet Navy's most important strategic role, to keep NATO out of the Norwegian Sea. The Norwegian fjords offered good cover for NATO ships wishing to target the Northern Fleet. The importance of the Baltic Straits and Turkish Straits dominated the thinking about the best use of naval-infantry assets associated with these fleet areas, too. With a commitment to supporting coastal defence also demanding attention, making a brigade-sized unit available for Soviet power projection would not be straightforward.

On a global level, the ability of naval infantry to project power across the world depended on carrier-borne air support. In the event, though, the ability

Recruitment and training

In the Soviet Union, males had to serve a term of compulsory military service when they reached 18. The naval-infantry brigades were seen as elite forces; those seeking to join needed to possess basic training in a speciality such as tanks, artillery, engineering, vehicle maintenance or radio communication, gained by attending clubs and summer camps while a cadet at school. When called up, individuals could indicate that they wished to join the naval infantry. Only volunteers would be accepted, though some with specific skills could be drafted from other branches of the Soviet Navy. Attributes such as physical fitness, sound morals, political reliability and an aggressive nature helped determine whether candidates would be successful. Recruits demonstrating to possess leadership abilities could be chosen to be NCOs following induction. Loyalty to the Communist Party, homeland and people was stressed. After basic training, the enlisted naval infantryman swore an oath of allegiance. Personal decorations with awards to the unit reinforced the branch's prestige, resulting in a high re-enlistment rate.

Initial training focused on the skills a motorized infantryman needed to possess. Then the training on board ship would begin with embarkation and disembarkation drills. Physical fitness, weapons training, map reading and land navigation would be covered, conducted amid hostile terrain and different environmental conditions. Basic training generally lasted four weeks and included weapons training. Political lessons taught the traditions of the naval infantry and the work of the Communist Party. A trainee was then assigned to a specific role depending upon the results of aptitude tests and experience gained as a cadet.

Unit training then began. The recruit learnt the importance of exercising initiative and independent action by training with small groups based on mutually supporting each other. Special training could include parachute jumping, working with demolitions and mines and operating in a snowy or marshy environment. Tactical exercises were conducted in conjunction with tanks, helicopter assaults, gun fire support from ships, and close air support. Obstacle courses with noise and light effects adding to the realism were employed. The most important exercise was the conduct of an operation to seize a beach or port. Practice landings and wartime operations were studied. The naval infantry received specialized training intended to prepare them for small independent unit operations as well as being deployed to spearhead a larger landing. Amphibious-vehicle crews practised manoeuvring their mount through water and firing its weapons while afloat. Combat engineers and demolition experts received special training to familiarize them with landing ships and smaller craft. Embarkation and disembarkation drills would be practised. Training was

to project power with lethal force would depend on land-based aircraft supporting the naval infantry, and lack of lift capacity would mean that amphibious operations could only be carried out close to home. This changed only slightly with the launching of the Kiev-class heavy aircraft cruisers. The deployment of the heavy aircraft cruiser *Kuznetsov* – launched in 1985, but not operational until December 1991 – was different because it could fly fixed-wing aircraft from its deck. A large flight deck and elevator did mean that larger helicopters could be operated; moreover, missile launchers on board could be used to attack land targets.

The capacity to carry up to 20 divisions existed, but was not discussed in detail in Soviet Navy doctrine. Auxiliary ships were built through the 1970s and could be used to support amphibious operations, though limited numbers and carrying capacity did not help. Soviet Navy doctrine did not envisage the use of commercial shipping to transport further follow-on ground forces. By the 1980s, commercial shipping could be called upon to assist with this task. During Soviet Navy exercises, such vessels would play the role of NATO ships bringing supplies to Europe and the target for interdiction.

When they envisaged a future conflict, Soviet strategic planners saw amphibious operations as being implicitly linked to the ground campaign. Admiral K.A. Stalbo advocated the use of tactical amphibious landings to support ground forces. Soviet doctrine specified five phases: preparation, sea movement, beach assault plus landing, achievement of mission, and withdrawal. It was deemed essential to plan an operation by assembling sufficiently trained forces and to centralize command and control to ensure the cooperation of all combat elements. Admiral A.P. Pronichkin

considered to be complete when the unit could conduct its own landing exercise.

NCOs, chosen from induction or once trained, completed six months of special training; if accepted, they would serve another year. Some then might go to college, graduate and return as officers. The *praporshchik* or ensign rank was open to those NCOs who re-enlisted for five years; they could then do a further stint, lasting either three or five years; at the age of 45 they joined the reserves. After ten years as an ensign the individual would be promoted lieutenant, or after five years if he had a certain job qualifying him for early promotion and had passed military tests.

The Nakhimov naval schools were the primary source of the naval infantry's officers, though this would change during the 1970s. A programme involving 220 hours of basic physical fitness and military skills was devised to provide military experiences to schoolboys; it was made compulsory from 1968. If boys aged 17–21 passed an entrance examination they could complete 6–8 weeks of basic training and join a military college. A special course for officers commissioned straight to the naval infantry was established at Kaliningrad by 1970, though graduates of any naval school could apply to join.

To train platoon commanders, by 1966 a naval-infantry faculty was created as part of the Higher Combined Arms School at Blagoveshchensk; a platoon of each cadet company was made up of naval infantry, and the first platoon commanders graduated in 1968. A naval-infantry faculty was established at the Leningrad Higher Command Arms Command School by 1989. Officers had to be taught to appreciate tactical problems; most of this was done on the job, but commanding officers established proper programmes and junior officers would be evaluated by superiors. An officer could attend a military school to update his specialist knowledge after he had completed two years' service.

By 1971, a naval-infantry officers' training centre was established at Sevastopol, teaching parachuting and reconnaissance specialists. Naval infantry who trained with parachutes received extra pay per jump. A 4½-month programme was developed and whole platoons which had recently taken the oath were sent there.

Officers typically spent three years as a *leytenánt* (lieutenant) and another three as a *stárshiy leytenánt* (senior lieutenant), four as a *kapitán* (captain), three as a *majór* (major), seven as a *podpolkóvnik* (lieutenant-colonel) and five as a *polkóvnik* (colonel). In the 1960s, most senior officers had fought in the naval infantry during the Great Patriotic War. Junior officers had comparative freedom to exercise their initiative, though some senior officers were prone to supervising them too closely.

stressed the importance of a ground force commander taking control of the landing, not the amphibious task force commander. The most modern communication equipment available would be used to facilitate coordination. The approach to the beach needed to be made with secrecy to achieve surprise. Communications security, dispersed embarkation points and night approaches would be employed to fool enemy commanders. The beach would be targeted by aircraft and gunfire before the landing. Fire-control parties would land to set up radio communications. Tactical air support would be coordinated through the command ship. Once the beachhead was secure, the naval infantry would be withdrawn; ground forces landed would continue the battle.

The purpose of amphibious operations might be for strategic effect, to seize the entrances to the Baltic Sea or Turkish Straits. Protecting the Northern Fleet's nuclear submarine bases would be difficult for motorized ground forces because of the harsh terrain, whereas naval infantry landed by ship on the Norwegian coast would facilitate a rapid seizure of important terrain.

Doctrine was practised and instilled by carrying out exercises. On 25 July 1967 a landing by Polnochny-class landing ships transporting PT-76 light tanks and BTR-60PB APCs was conducted near Leningrad. Exercise *Sever-68* saw the naval infantry carry out amphibious landings on the Baltic coast and the Rybachy Peninsula in conjunction with other Warsaw Pact troops; the naval infantry played NATO aggressors to be defeated by Warsaw Pact ground forces. Exercise *Okean-70* involved two battalions of naval infantry landing on the Rybachy Peninsula; the naval infantry took the beach, followed up by ground forces tasked with exploitation. A second landing, on a Baltic island supposedly targeted by a nuclear weapon, was also carried out. Exercise *Yug-71*, involving the Moskva-class helicopter carrier *Leningrad*, saw the 810th Separate Marine Brigade land near Odessa.

Seven merchant ships with naval infantry on board participated in Exercise *Okean-75*, while Exercise *Shchit-76* saw a brigade-sized landing on the Baltic coast in which eight landing ships participated alongside Warsaw Pact forces. Exercise *Val-77* would see hovercraft land naval infantry at the same time as helicopters, with guided-missile boats supporting the landings with gunfire and smoke screens; APCs would only disembark troops when determined enemy force was met.

Exercise *Bratstvo po oruzhiyu-80* saw naval infantry conduct a beach landing during a wider set of ground exercises. Infantry was deployed by helicopter before ships landed troops on the beach; they then attacked a nearby airfield in conjunction with East German airborne forces. The force then captured a port.

The Northern Fleet's 61st Separate Marine Brigade participated in Exercise *Zapad-81*, the largest ever conducted by Soviet forces; it saw the debut of the heavy aircraft cruiser *Kiev*. As well as providing the military

F

NAVAL INFANTRY ON EXERCISE, 1960s
(1) RPD gunner, summer uniform

This naval infantryman wears summer uniform: black beret with a black jacket worn over his sleeveless striped undershirt, black breeches and black knee-boots. A small gold anchor on a red flag was worn on the left side of the beret. On the front of the beret enlisted men wore a small red star. The infantry badge is displayed on the left sleeve of his jacket. On the jacket shoulder boards, enlisted men wore a two-letter designation, the fleet initials and rank insignia. The lettering on this man's shoulder straps indicates that he is with the Baltic Fleet. Enlisted men wore a black, artificial-leather belt with a large front plate with fleet insignia embossed on it. When appropriate, the Guards emblem was worn on the right front side of the jacket, with military ribbons and decorations on the left side above the breast pockets.

Work on the 7.62mm RPD light machine gun began during the Great Patriotic War. It used two 50-round belts, linked together, from its drum. The safety catch was positioned just ahead of the trigger and pivoted through 180 degrees. Fully automatic was the only mode. The RPD was a bulky weapon, but a good and stable platform for prolonged firing. Rounds would be pushed through the front of the belt and not first pulled out of the belt before being pushed forward. Production ran from 1948–60. Effective range was up to 1,000m.

(2) Naval infantryman, winter uniform

This naval infantryman wears the winter uniform, which was the same as the summer uniform but with a heavy black jacket with a fur collar; a black fur cap and black gloves could also be worn, and a black greatcoat with an anchor emblem on the upper left arm was available. For landing and combat exercises a helmet with a red star on the front could be worn. This man wears the SSh-60 helmet, similar outwardly to the SSh-40 worn during the Great Patriotic War, though the former had four not three stuffed leather pads for comfort.

A personal kit bag with mess kit, rations, and rain poncho was carried; the greatcoat could be attached on top. A water

bottle and entrenching tool (both with covers), grenade pouch, plus ammunition pouch for either three magazines or one large machine-gun magazine completed his equipment, weighing 25–30kg. A loose-fitting camouflage or white coverall for summer or winter training was also issued. Fur-lined boots and heavy gloves would be used for Arctic training.

The 7.62mm AKM assault rifle he carries was issued from 1959 in place of the 7.62mm AK-47 assault rifle; the newer weapon weighed 1kg less and had greater accuracy. The AKM could be fired in either semi-automatic or full-automatic mode; its cyclic rate was 600rd/min. Its wooden stock housed a cleaning kit; 30-round magazines were issued but 40-round box magazines and 75-round RPK drum magazines could also be used. Effective range was 350m.

(3) BRDM-1 crewman

This man wears the usual gear issued to vehicle crews, teamed with the customary striped undershirt. His helmet is connected to the R-124 intercom system by a cable. The BRDM-1 was a four-wheeled armoured amphibious scout car produced during 1957–66. The Model 1957 had an open roof while the Model 1958 had a roof with two hatches; neither vehicle model had any armament. The Model 1959, the standard production model, had a 7.62mm SGMB MMG mounted on a front pintle. The Model 1960, shown here, had two additional pintle mounts for optional SGMBs. The BRDM-1's maximum armour thickness was only 10mm, sufficient to protect its crew from small-arms fire only. A single rear-mounted water jet propelled the vehicle through water. A trim board was raised at the front for stability before the vehicle entered water. Four auxiliary belly wheels could be used to help deal with trenches. The BRDM-1 was designed as a purpose-built armoured car for reconnaissance work, but if the crew closed the hatches they could not operate the armament. This drawback led to the design of the BRDM-2, which sported a turret mounting a 14.5mm KPVT HMG and a coaxial 7.62mm PKT GPMG.

Pictured in February 1983, this is the Kiev-class heavy aircraft cruiser *Minsk*. Commissioned in 1975–82, the three ships of this class – *Kiev*, *Minsk* and *Novorossiysk* – could deploy up to 12 Yakoviev Yak-38 VTOL strike fighters. These VTOL aircraft had a limited bomb load, however, and their comparatively poor manoeuvrability meant they could not compete with NATO fighters. The presence of a large flight deck and elevator meant larger helicopters, Kamov Ka-25 or Ka-27, could be operated with naval infantry on board. Missile launchers on board could be used to attack land targets. (SSGT GLENN LINDSEY/Wikimedia/Public Domain)

personnel involved with valuable experience, the exercise served to remind the citizens of Poland and other Warsaw Pact countries of the Soviet Union's military might at a time of growing unrest and dissatisfaction with life under communism.

Exercise *Shchit-82* involved naval infantry landing by helicopter and boat, followed by Soviet Army motorized troops. In Exercise *Shchit-83*, the 810th Separate Marine Brigade's airborne and reconnaissance battalions landed by parachute at the same time as a beach landing at night. The incompatible communication systems of the three services – Navy, Air Force, Army – made coordination during difficult. Soviet doctrine specified that landing areas were to be up to 13km apart to exclude the possibility of a nuclear weapon affecting both. Cargoes were distributed across different ships of the same class so if some sank then others had the equipment needed. A naval-infantry brigade could be carried by three landing detachments departing from separate locations, while a landing support detachment and an escort detachment to guard the landing detachments from enemy ships or submarines were also deployed. Fighter-bomber aircraft aboard ships of the landing support detachment would be the first to be committed to battle, tasked with suppressing the enemy defences near the landing site; the landing ships' approach route would then be guarded. Tactical nuclear weapons could be used.

A landing beach 200–300km from the front line would be chosen because it had to be supported by land-based aircraft. Airborne troops would land to isolate the landing area from enemy reserve forces. While a motor-rifle division made a landing on a front of 20–30km, a naval-infantry brigade would be assigned a landing site up to 10km wide, with an individual battalion given a sector 2km wide. Tactical deployment of the landing ships occurred 20–25nmi from shore; ships would follow each other to the coast. Some 30–40 minutes before the landing, helicopters would deploy soldiers to the landing beaches. Hovercraft would be the first to land. Minesweeper helicopters would assist specialist engineers in clearing passages. The naval-infantry brigade would seize the landing point and move to 4–6km inland. To assist with rapid unloading, a floating berth with ramp would be set up on the beach and a metal road surface would be laid.

WEAPONS AND EQUIPMENT

The assault rifle used by the naval infantry in the 1960s and 1970s was the 7.62mm AKM, replaced from the late 1970s by the 5.45mm AK-74; each squad also had a 7.62mm RPK LMG, similarly supplanted by the 5.45mm RPK-74. A 7.62mm SVD marksman rifle, feeding from a ten-round box magazine, was issued to each section; its 4x PSO-1 telescopic sight gave it an effective range of 800m.

Naval infantrymen also carried the RKG-3M anti-tank hand grenade with a high-explosive anti-tank (HEAT) warhead and the RGD-5 anti-personnel fragmentation hand grenade. The RPG-7 rocket-propelled grenade launcher had an effective range of 300m and could defeat 330mm of armour; rate of fire was 4–6rd/min. The RPG-26 single-shot, disposable anti-tank rocket launcher was used from the 1980s and was capable of penetrating 440mm of armour; the RPG-27, issued from 1989, could penetrate 660mm of armour.

The 9K32 Strela-2 and 9K32M Strela-2M SAMs, issued by 1968 and 1970 respectively and designed to be used as man-portable air-defence systems (MANPADS), were used by the naval infantry. They used heat-seeking missiles armed with fragmentation warheads to target enemy aircraft. The 9K38 Igla and 9K310 Igla-1 MANPADS, issued from 1983 and 1981 respectively, had better operational ranges and improved sensors.

Company-level support weapons included the 7.62mm PK GPMG with bipod or the 7.62mm PKS GPMG with tripod; both weapons had an effective range of 1,000m, used 50-round ammunition belts in 100-, 200- or 250-round boxes and offered a rate of fire of 650rd/min. The 82mm mortar would be at the company commander's disposal. At battalion level the 82mm B-10 recoilless rifle had an effective range of 400m and a rate of fire of 5–7rd/min.

Wheeled APCs used by the naval infantry included the BRDM-1 amphibious wheeled armoured scout car and later the BRDM-2. Production of the BTR-60, the first fully amphibious wheeled APC, started by 1960; it could carry 14 passengers and two crew, but it had an open roof, which made it particularly vulnerable. A 7.62mm SGMB MMG was mounted near the front hatch, but the weapon was replaced by the 7.62mm PK GPMG on the

The RGD-5 anti-personnel fragmentation grenade entered Soviet service in the 1950s and has been widely exported. This example is fitted with a UZRGM fuze. (Ulmosto/Wikimedia/CC BY-SA 3.0)

Naval infantry equipped with AK-74 assault rifles are pictured during training: they might be tackling an obstacle course, certainly an important part of training for most amphibious infantry. The setting suggests a hot climate where black clothing was resented by most as the garments did nothing to keep out the heat. (AirSeaLand Photos)

Throughout the 1970s and 1980s the Soviet marine brigade lacked organic towed or self-propelled artillery support assets. The battalion commander could only call upon his mortar platoon and the MRL battery, a brigade-level asset. This MRL battery was equipped with the 122mm BM-21 Grad MRL depicted here; in this photograph the battery commander, a *mayor* holding a map and a pair of binoculars, is flanked by two crewmen. The BM-21's 40 rocket tubes could lay down a devastating barrage, but its fire could not be adjusted once started. (AirSeaLand Photos)

BTR-60PA, which featured a fully enclosed hull. The BTR-60PA could carry 14 passengers; operational range was 500km. Produced during 1966–87, the eight-wheeled BTR-60PB had a turret-mounted 14.5mm KPVT HMG and a coaxial 7.62mm PKT GPMG; the vehicle had a closed top and a crew of two, with capacity for only eight passengers. The BTR-60PB was partially replaced in the 1970s by the similarly equipped eight-wheeled BTR-70 APC and then the eight-wheeled BTR-80 amphibious APC from the mid-1980s, both types having three crew and capacity for seven passengers.

Tracked APCs included the BTR-50PK amphibious carrier, which carried 20 passengers and two crew and had a 7.62mm SGMB MMG; it remained in service into the late 1970s. By the 1980s, BMP amphibious tracked infantry fighting vehicles (IFVs) were used by the naval infantry alongside the wheeled types outlined above. The BMP-1 and BMP-2, available in several variants, had a turret-mounted 73mm 2A28 Grom semi-automatic gun with 40 rounds (24 HEAT and 16 high-explosive) plus a 7.62mm PKT GPMG with 2,000 rounds and a mount for the 9M14 Malyutka wire-guided ATGM; this system could also be fitted to the BRDM-2.

G **NAVAL INFANTRY ON OPERATIONS, 1970s**
(1) Naval infantryman, 1970s
He wears an SSh-68 helmet with net and a KLMK camouflage hooded suit over his naval-infantry jacket and trousers. He carries a 7.62mm AKM assault rifle and wears a water bottle, magazine pouch and grenade pouch on his waist belt.
(2) RPK gunner, 1970s
He wears KZS camouflage trousers and jacket, issued from 1975. The KZS uniform was designed with a limited life expectancy, fabricated from loose-weave cotton fabric. He is equipped with a 7.62mm RPK LMG, produced during 1961–78. AKM magazines could be used, but 40-round boxes or a 75-round drum were common. Cyclic rate was 600rd/min and effective range (in conjunction with the bipod) was 800m.
(3) *Mayor*, naval infantry
The major wears standard naval-infantry uniform with a beret

featuring an officers' badge with gold braid surrounding the star, hammer and sickle. Unlike enlisted men's shoulder straps, officers' shoulder boards designated rank only. Officers had a black artificial-leather belt with a shoulder strap but no front plate. He has a holstered 9mm Makarov PM semi-automatic pistol and a map case on his belt. The PM was a light weapon for self-defence and had an eight-round magazine.

The PT-76 amphibious light tank issued to the naval infantry carried a 76mm D-56T gun with 40 rounds and could fire 6–8rd/min; effective range was 1,500m. Usually, 24 high-explosive fragmentation rounds, eight armour-piercing rounds and eight high-explosive anti-tank rounds would be carried. Operational range on land was 400km, or 500km with external fuel tanks. Armour was comparatively weak, with only 25mm on the turret front. The PT-76 could reach speeds of 44km/h on the road.

Drawn up in three ranks, these naval infantrymen wear berets and overalls bearing vehicle designations. Most of the men are probably crew for the PT-76 amphibious light tanks visible behind them. The PT-76 only had a three-man crew, with the commander also being the gunner and radio operator. (AirSeaLand Photos)

Naval-infantry tank units were equipped with the T-54/55 MBT and the PT-76 amphibious light tank. The MRL battalions of the Soviet naval infantry were equipped with the 122mm BM-21 Grad truck-mounted MRL.

In Soviet Navy service, much use was made of LCUs (see table below). While naval-infantry brigades were ideally equipped for quick, mobile actions, their lack of a logistical 'tail' would prevent them from carrying out sustained operations. The small size of the landing craft available also limited the operational range of such activities. While Soviet Navy assets could transport up to 20,000–25,000 men if concentrated, the US military could embark 130,000 Marines.

PT-76 amphibious light tanks and a PTS-M amphibious transport come ashore from a Ropucha-class landing ship. With a standard displacement of 2,200 long tons, the Ropucha-class vessels were capable of 18kn (33km/h) and had a range of 6,000nmi (11,112km) at 15kn (28km/h). Equipped with both bow and stern doors, they could carry a variety of loads including ten MBTs and 340 infantrymen or 500 tons of cargo. (AirSeaLand Photos)

Ivan Rogov was one of three landing ships in its class commissioned between 1978 and 1990. Displacing 13,000 tons fully loaded, the ship was launched by 1978, followed by two others (1982 and 1988). Operational range was 7,500nmi (13,890km) at 14kn (26km/h). A battalion of naval infantry with ten T-55 MBTs and 30 APCs could be carried. Four assault helicopters could be also operated from its deck, though four Ka-25 or Ka-32 ASW helicopters was the usual complement. Two Kalmar-class LCACs would also be carried. (US gov/Wikimedia/Public Domain)

Soviet Navy LCUs			
Type	Number launched	Capacity	Maximum speed
MP-2	23	200 tons – 200 men or 4 APCs	16kn (30km/h)
MP-4	10	800 tons – 6–8 tanks	12kn (22km/h)
MP-6	8	500 tons – 6–10 tanks	12kn (22km/h)
MP-8	19	400 tons – 6–8 tanks, 5 BRDMs or 10 BTRs	15kn (28km/h)
MP-10	c.40	150 tons – 4 tanks	–
SMB-1	30	200 tons – 4 tanks	10kn (18.5km/h)

The Soviet Navy also employed Tapir-class landing ships – a type known as the 'Alligator' in the West – with 14 entering service during 1966–75. With a standard displacement of 3,400 long tons, these vessels could carry 300–425 troops plus 20 tanks or 40 AFVs, or 1,000 long tons of supplies. Larger vessels included the Polnochny-class landing ship and the Ivan Rogov-class landing ship. Displacing 800–1,150 long tons when fully loaded, the Polnochny-class ships could carry ten APCs, four MBTs or 250 infantrymen; they had an operational range of 1,000nmi (1,852km) at 18kn (33km/h).

As well as landing craft, the Soviet Navy used air-cushioned vehicles. The Gus-class LCAC, displacing 27 long tons, could carry 50 passengers or 25 infantrymen with equipment; operational range was 230nmi (426km) at 43kn (80km/h) or 185nmi (343km) at 50kn (93km/h). Built during 1970–85, the larger Aist-class LCAC had a standard displacement of 310 long tons, a maximum speed of 70kn (130km/h) and a range of 120nmi (222km) at

This Kalmar-class LCAC was photographed in 1985. With 20 completed during 1972–85, the Kalmar-class LCACs, known as the 'Lebed' in the West, could carry a T-55 MBT, two PT-76 amphibious light tanks, two BTR-60/70 APCs or 120 infantry. (US gov/Wikimedia/Public Domain)

50kn (93km/h); it could carry two T-55 MBTs and 200 infantrymen, four PT-76 amphibious light tanks and 50 infantryman, or three APCs and 100 infantrymen. The Kalmar-class LCAC could achieve a maximum speed of 55kn (102km/h) and had an operational range of 100nmi (185km) at 50kn (93km/h). The largest LCAC type used by the Soviet Navy, displacing 555 long tons fully loaded, was the Zubr-class ('Pomornik') LCAC; 15 were built during 1987–90. Maximum speed was 63kn (117km/h) and operational range was 300nmi (556km) at 55kn (102km/h); the type could carry 500 troops, three MBTs, ten APCs/IFVs with 140 troops, or eight APCs or amphibious tanks.

H NAVAL INFANTRY ON EXERCISE, 1980s

(1) RPK-74 gunner, 1980s

This naval infantryman wears the TTsKO woodland-pattern camouflage cotton trousers and jacket issued from 1982. He is equipped with a 5.45mm RPK-74 LMG. Cyclic rate is 600rd/min and effective range is 1,000m. Unlike the RPK, the RPK-74 has a box magazine holding 45 rounds; 30-round AKM magazines can also be used with the weapon. His magazine pouch holds four magazines.

(2) Naval infantryman in winter gear, 1980s

This man is wearing the winter TTsKO woodland-pattern camouflage trousers and jacket with an *ushanka* cap. He is equipped with a 5.45mm AKS-74U, an SMG model of the 5.45mm AK-74 assault rifle produced from 1979. With an effective range of 200m, it can be used in conjunction with 30-round AK-74 magazines or 45-round RPK-74 magazines. With the folding stock extended it is only 735mm long; the AK-74 with stock out is 943mm long. He wears pouches on his waist belt for F-1 anti-personnel fragmentation hand grenades and 30-round AK-74 magazines.

(3) Naval infantryman with grenade launcher, 1980s

This naval infantryman wears an SSh-68 helmet with light TTsKO woodland-pattern camouflage trousers and jacket. He is equipped with an AK-74 with a 40mm GP-25 grenade launcher fitted under the barrel. Produced from 1978, the GP-25 can be used with both the AKM and AK-74. The lightened GP-30 was issued by 1989 to complement the GP-25. The 40mm grenade has no case as the base of the grenade has both propellant and primer, so there is no need to extract a cartridge before another grenade is loaded. The grenade could go off when it is loaded, though the fuze would not be armed until the grenade flies 10–40m, limiting the damage this could cause. Sights are on the left side of the GP-25, with an indirect firing scale for longer ranges up to 400m. Effective range is 100–150m. He wears a pouch for his 30-round AK-74 magazines.

OPERATIONS

The naval infantry would deploy around the world on operations to assist socialist regimes that had gained independence from colonial powers. The availability of larger landing ships made such deployments possible and tested the ability of the naval infantry to influence political crises.

In 1967, the 309th Separate Marine Battalion deployed to Port Said, Egypt, aboard two large and two medium landing ships. On 10 July 1967, a landing detachment of the 61st Separate Marine Regiment was sent from Pechenga to the Mediterranean, composed of a company of marines, a PT-76 company, a T-54 company and a platoon of marines in BTR-60s; they stayed until 1 October that year. Another detachment of similar size with a ZSU-23-4 Shilka SPAAG battery and an ATGM battery was sent from October 1967 to February 1968. In May 1970, the 810th Separate Marine Regiment carried out exercises off the Egyptian coast. A battalion from the regiment took part in exercises with Syrian forces during 1981.

During February–July 1972 a battalion of naval infantry plus a tank company and an engineer platoon were sent to Guinea in West Africa, where President Ahmed Sékou Touré had set up a socialist republic. In 1975, civil war broke out in Angola; with Moscow keen to exert its influence on the People's Movement for the Liberation of Angola (MPLA), one of the factions involved, Soviet naval infantry deployed to Conakry, the capital of Guinea, were able to sail to Luanda on the Angolan coast. During early 1977 a detachment from the 61st Separate Marine Regiment sailed to Luanda to demonstrate Soviet support. During the 1980s, in response to Angolan requests for Soviet assistance in the face of the deployment of South African forces in Angola, the 336th Separate Guards Marine Regiment sent detachments to that country; the nature of the support the detachments gave the MPLA is unclear, however.

Naval infantry of the 55th Marine Division were sent on frequent assignments to the Indian and Pacific oceans, as the Soviet Union intervened in the febrile relationships between Ethiopia, Eritrea, Somalia, Yemen and other countries. In November 1977, the naval infantry helped to protect Soviet civilians and equipment during the evacuation of Mogadishu, the capital of Somalia; in the following year they protected personnel being evacuated from the Soviet base at Berbera in Somalia, and a tank platoon landed to help Ethiopian forces seize the Eritrean port of Massawa.

Also in 1977, Soviet landing ships assisted South Yemeni forces in the occupation of Socotra and other coastal islands. On 2 February 1980, *Ivan Rogov* and the Tapir-class landing ship *Nikolai Vilkov* embarked Ka-25 and Ka-27 helicopters, Kalmar-class LCACs and 300 naval infantrymen from the 165th and 390th Marine regiments and set off from Vladivostok to the Indian Ocean. By the end of April 1980, the naval infantry had started to prepare for a landing exercise on Socotra in conjunction with South Yemeni marines; the Soviet troops were issued blank ammunition, but also carried live ammunition just in case anything went wrong with the South Yemeni militia on the island who were to play the 'enemy' force. The Kalmar-class LCACs departed the *Nikolai Vilkov* 5km from the coast and PT-76 amphibious light tanks were offloaded 1,000m from the shoreline; tanks, BMPs and BTRs stayed near the coast while Soviet sappers made safe passages on land and helicopters landed troops on high points. When mines were detonated mistakenly, the South Yemeni militia leapt from their trenches and ran.

Two patterns of camouflage employed by the naval infantry in the Cold War period. Above is the KLMK (*Kamuflirovannyy Letniy Maskirovochnyy Kombinezon*, 'camouflaged summer deceptive coverall') pattern worn from the late 1960s; below is one variation of the TTsKO (*tryokhtsvetnaya kamuflirovannaya odezhda*, 'three colour camouflage') pattern worn from the early 1980s. (Militarist/Alamy Stock Photo)

As South Yemen descended into civil war in the early 1980s, a battalion-strength force drawn from the 390th Marine Regiment was located on Nokra Island off the Eritrean coast. The 882nd Marine Battalion from the 810th Separate Marine Brigade was also sent there, and practised a landing on the island to see if it was possible to capture it from an enemy occupying force. After the discovery of oil on the border of North and South Yemen led to unification of the countries on 22 May 1990, the Soviet assistance programme came to an end.

Soviet naval-infantry detachments were also sent to Vietnam's Cam Ranh naval base, built by the United States during the Vietnam War. Seeking to advertise Soviet military might in the region, ships of the Soviet Navy's Pacific Fleet including the Kiev-class heavy aircraft cruiser *Minsk* used the

Soviet naval infantrymen conduct a demonstration for visiting US Navy personnel, September 1990. (PHCS Mitchell/Wikimedia/Public Domain)

base from 1979 onwards. A battalion from the 55th Marine Division was sent to Cam Ranh Bay during October 1984 and conducted landing exercises on the Vietnamese coast. Deploying from the Ivan Rogov-class landing ship *Aleksandr Nikolayev* in heavy fog, two companies of naval infantry mounted on BTR-60PBs and two PT-76 platoons of the 165th Marine Regiment landed on the beach at the designated places.

Photographed in September 1990, these Soviet naval infantrymen are staging a hand-to-hand combat demonstration during a military review. (PH1 Ted Salois, U.S. Navy/Wikimedia/Public Domain)

AFTERMATH

In the years after the fall of the Soviet Union, the naval infantry would be deployed by Russia as elite infantry, notably in the First and Second Chechen wars (1994–96 and 1999–2009 respectively). In early January 1995, the 336th Separate Marine Brigade, based at Kaliningrad, sent the 879th Marine Airborne Battalion to Chechnya. The battalion deployed for up to two months, fighting for critical locations in Grozny, the capital city, and sustained 97 casualties. The 165th Marine Regiment deployed to Chechnya from January to May 1995; the 61st Separate Guards Marine Brigade's 876th Marine Airborne Battalion, part of Russia's high-readiness force, also fought in Grozny from January 1995, staying until 26 June and losing 64 men killed. The 336th Separate Marine Brigade deployed the 877th Marine Battalion to Chechnya between early May and late June, fighting alongside the Pacific Fleet's 106th Marine Regiment.

The First Chechen War led to the withdrawal of Russian forces from Chechnya by 31 December 1996; Chechen independence was recognized by January 1997. In response to Chechen fighters raiding Dagestan, the Russian republic neighbouring Chechnya, the Russian Federation launched a ground attack on Grozny on 30 September 1999, marking the beginning of the Second Chechen War. This time, ground forces spearheaded the Russian operation with the naval infantry playing a supporting role. The 876th Marine Airborne Battalion returned to Chechnya, reinforced with a mortar battery, a 2S1 self-propelled artillery battery and a single ATGM battery. Fielding a full complement of APCs, the battalion served in Chechnya until June 2000, losing 16 men killed. After major military operations in Chechnya came to an end, anti-guerrilla operations continued; the 414th and 727th Separate Marine battalions from the Caspian Sea Flotilla helped with these operations.

From 2000 onwards, Russian marine units underwent changes to their designations and missions. Assigned to the Pacific Fleet, the 40th Separate Marine Brigade was established on 6 August 2007 from the 40th Separate Motorized Rifle Brigade. On 1 December 2009, the 155th Separate Marine Brigade was established from the Pacific Fleet's disbanded 55th Marine Division. The 61st Separate Marine Brigade deployed units to the Donbass

Russian marines training in Sevastopol, September 2008. After the collapse of the Soviet Union, conscripts serving in the Russian Federation's ground forces suffered from poor morale, a dearth of competent officers, bad equipment and limited training. By contrast, Russian marines had a high proportion of professional soldiers among the conscripts, the best equipment the Russian military possessed, effective combat training and experienced officers. They took on a disproportionate burden of the fighting in Chechnya, especially during the urban battle for Grozny in January 1995. (Antoine Gyori/AGP/Corbis via Getty Images)

The Russian Tapir-class landing ship *Nikolay Filchenkov* passes through the Bosphorus Strait off Istanbul, believed to be on its way to the Syrian port city of Tartus, October 2016. Elements of Soviet-era equipment and fleet assets such as this vessel, in service since the 1970s, have continued in Russian service to the present day. (OZAN KOSE/AFP via Getty Images)

region to assist Russian separatists during 2014 and to Syria during 2016, helping Syrian forces to take Palmyra from Islamic State on 27 March 2016.

The 40th and 155th Separate Marine brigades both deployed units on ground operations against Ukraine during 2022. Only the 810th Separate Marine Brigade stood ready to launch amphibious landings on the Ukrainian coast, however, as both the 61st and the 336th Separate Marine brigades deployed battalion tactical groups on ground operations in northern Ukraine.

BIBLIOGRAPHY

Anonymous (1984). *The Soviet Army: Specialized Warfare and Rear Area Support*. FM 100-2-2. Washington, DC: Headquarters, Department of the Army. Available at https://irp.fas.org/doddir/army/fm100-2-2.pdf

Carroll, J. (1977). *Soviet Naval Infantry* (Report number ADA 047604). Available at https://apps.dtic.mil/sti/citations/ADA047604

Clifford, D. (1971). *Soviet Naval Infantry: A new capability?* (ADA 951638). Available at https://apps.dtic.mil/sti/citations/ADA951638

Kabanov, S. (1977). *Pole boiia-bereg* [The Battlefield is the Shore]. Moscow: Voenizdat.

Kamalov, Kh.Kh. (1966). *Morskaia pekhota v boiakh za rodinu* [Naval Infantry in battles for the Motherland]. Moscow: Voenizdat.

Lewis, E. (1977). *A Comprehensive Examination of the Soviet Naval Infantry* (Report number 0480186). Available at http://apps.dtic.mil/sti/citations/ADA048186

Pavlov, A.S. (1997). *Warships of the USSR and Russia, 1945–1995*. Annapolis, MD: Naval Institute Press.

Pestanov, S.A. (1976). *Soldaty morskoi pekhoty* [Soldiers of the Naval Infantry]. Petrozavadsk: Karelia.

Ranft, B. & Till, G. (1983). *The Sea in Soviet Naval Strategy*. Annapolis, MD: Naval Institute Press.

Sharp, Charles (1995). *Red Death: Soviet Order of Battle World War II, Volume VII: Mountain, Naval, NKVD and Allied Divisions and Brigades 1941 to 1945*. West Chester, PA: The Nafziger Collection.

Watson, B. & S. (1986). *The Soviet Navy: Strengths and Liabilities*. London: Arms & Armour Press.

INDEX